TIMBER HOMES

Taking Wood to New Levels

The Deutsche Nationalbibliothek lists this publication in the Deutsche Nationalbibliografie; detailed bibliographic data are available on the Internet at http://dnb.dnb.de

ISBN 978-3-03768-282-1

www.braun-publishing.ch

1st edition 2023

Project coordination: Editorial office van Uffelen
Editorial staff and layout: Julia Kurkin, Lara Stoller, Dorian van Uffelen, Jacqueline Wenger
Graphic concept: Michaela Prinz, Berlin
Reproduction: Bild1Druck GmbH, Berlin

Chris van Uffelen

TIMBER HOMES

Taking Wood to New Levels

BRAUN

CONTENT

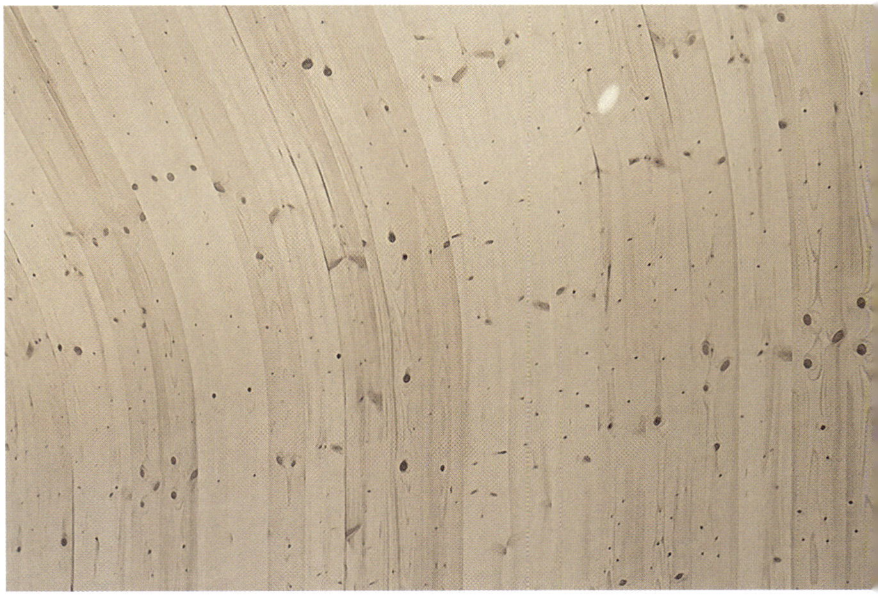

$6\ H_2O + 6\ CO_2 = C_6H_{12}O_6 + 6\ O_2$

Wood as a building material is on everyone's tongue again today. This was not always the case, but it was for a long time. After all, wood was used as a building material at the beginning of numerous advanced civilizations. Although the effect that early timber construction had on the natural stone construction that usually followed is often overestimated, timber construction remained involved in building activity in many places for centuries. Not only in regions where there was a lack of stone did timber offer the possibility of fast and comparatively cheap construction. Beams made it easy to span large rooms without vaulting, and roof trusses could be built more or less at the drop of a hat in this particular light and adaptable material. Wood was not always used only in its aged state, as the adaptability of the still moist and thus "intelligent" material was exploited for complex constructions. Traditionally, different types of timber construction can be distinguished: The simplest forms are log construction as a stacking of logs or beams on top of each other, and post and beam construction as a row next to each other. Half-timbered construction is a form of frame construction in which the uprights connected at the top and bottom by a beam (sill/peg) are spaced so far apart that they have to be fixed in place by further short ledgers and diagonal braces. The self-supporting timber frame is then filled with any material or boarded up. Timber truss techniques are already documented from the Neolithic Age.

These basic principles have remained largely unchanged to this day, and even when solid stone construction has long since dominated architecture, the traditional timber construction has remained a prominent feature of the townscape. In many places, "modern" Renaissance palaces and Baroque churches can be found among wooden townhouses, and in some contemporary metropolises, such as Paris or Amsterdam, individual wooden buildings have survived to this day. For constructive tasks in invisible places, the roof truss, for example, wood remained a preferred material, even if the 13th century already used metal for complex solutions (ring anchor of the Sainte-Chapelle in Paris). A typical feature of traditional half-timbered construction is the increasing cantilevering of the stories upwards, so that the walls stand as a counter-load to the weight on the floors, outside the story below: Thus, timber frame construction has long been used to create buildings up to seven stories high, with heights of 25–30 meters. Wood remained the preferred building material for story floors until well into the 19th century and for roof trusses until today.

The main argument against wood is probably its combustibility. Wood ignites at around 230 °C, at 260 °C wood burns even without an external heat source and at 400 °C the wood gases ignite themselves. However, buildings today can be calculated to burn down and some wooden beams can withstand heat longer than a softening steel beam. Heat treatment, which gives wood new properties, is a new technique that is currently driving timber construction forward (Thermally Modified Timber, TMT). However, the development of Cross Laminated Timber (CLT) seems to have a revolutionary effect on timber construction: As strong and fire-resistant as structural steel or concrete, various high-rise buildings are currently being planned with these bonded board layers.

However, there are other reasons why wood is so popular again today – especially for living: ecological and psychological reasons and questions of building biology. First of all, wood affects the mind with its natural surface and warmth, but also with its visual qualities of grain, aging and color. Measurements in different workrooms showed that those equipped with wooden furniture had the lowest electrical conductivity of the skin as a stress indicator. In classrooms with solid wood the heart rate variability of the students decreased when they entered. Numerous other studies show the positive effect of wood on well-being and even on the assessment of competence and friendliness. The material thus has psychological properties that go beyond the purely physical qualities of optics and materials.

In addition, quality wood is also advantageous from a building biology point of view: Wood creates a pleasant and healthy indoor climate. With the deposited dry used building material, the new building moisture and thus the mold risk is immediately eliminated, so vapor retarders are cleanly executed. But with the ability to absorb and release moisture, open-pored wood becomes a natural air conditioner. It also binds odors. On the other hand, one hears again and again about the exceeding of the wood-based indoor air quality standards by natural volatile organic compounds (NVOCs), which must be taken into account in wood construction through the selection of building materials. Ventilation in case of wood odor (terpenes) is the remedy of choice. Another building quality is that wood feels warm to the touch. This is due to the fact that it does not conduct heat particularly well and therefore insulates heat better as a building material than steel, glass or concrete.

The ecological balance sheet is probably the most positive argument for timber construction of all. No other building material can already show a climate-positive balance in its production. As it grows, a tree binds carbon dioxide from the air and uses its carbon and water in photosynthesis as a building material, while it releases oxygen into the atmosphere. As long as it exists as wood – i. e. it neither decays nor burns – it also remains bound. Wood consists of about half carbon. For one kilogram of wood, about 1.55 kilograms of carbon dioxide are consumed, and in one cubic meter of wood the carbon of about one ton of carbon dioxide is stored. Thus, an average Finnish single-family house made of wood sequesters about 30 tons of carbon dioxide from the air – ideally, it does this for a few centuries while other trees grow for more houses. That's why wood construction is now being touted as a carbon sink against the climate crisis that can at least help us in our attempt to reach the Paris Climate Agreement goals, ratified in 2016, to limit global warming. Physicist Hans Joachim Schellnhuber, Director Emeritus of the Potsdam Institute for Climate Impact Research (PIK), is one of the main proponents of this idea, which he is trying to promote with the "Bauhaus of the Earth" (Bauhaus Earth).

In addition, wood as a building material already has a very good energy balance when it is manufactured from the raw material tree, especially since the energy used for this purpose is often obtained from the by-products such as the bark. In fact, more energy is generated than consumed in the manufacture of conventional timber products. Starting from this basis, wood is also used in sustainable building techniques. For example, when it is used as a decomposable structure in cradle-to-cradle construction: the material is to be installed in such a way that it can be dismantled into its basic components at any time, i. e. pure assembly, no gluing whatsoever, and certainly not indissolubly. If a record is then kept of the elements used (Madaster, BIM), the completed building can be a kind of "reserve account" for the builder as the value of the materials that will one day be released again.

Timber construction will therefore probably continue to be a growing market, despite all the considerations, not least because people feel good in it. This is also shown by the examples presented to the reader in this volume. Buildings and rooms that offer the inhabitants an atmosphere and lifestyle.

HOME//OFFICE
JÜBEK, GERMANY

This new live/work space in Jübek, Northern Germany prioritizes ample daylighting and the use of natural materials. Located directly on Große Straße, the village's main street, adjacent to a nursery, café, and single-family house, the building's central location required contextual sensitivity.

The rectangular, gabled form of the building is based on the typical farmhouses of the region and follows the elongated site. An open gable facing the street reveals activity within the southern double-height workspace. The bending shields a private garden and terrace at the back of the property while also inviting visitors towards the glazed central entrance. The northern, taller of the two volumes, houses the kitchen, bathroom, meeting, work and sleeping rooms.

The walls and roof form a monolithic shell of larch wood cladding on the exterior and white clay plaster on the inside. The strategic placement of openings and the use of light, warm finishes create an interior flooded with daylight. Renewable building materials like wood and cellulose insulation reduce the building's ecological footprint and create a comfortable indoor climate.

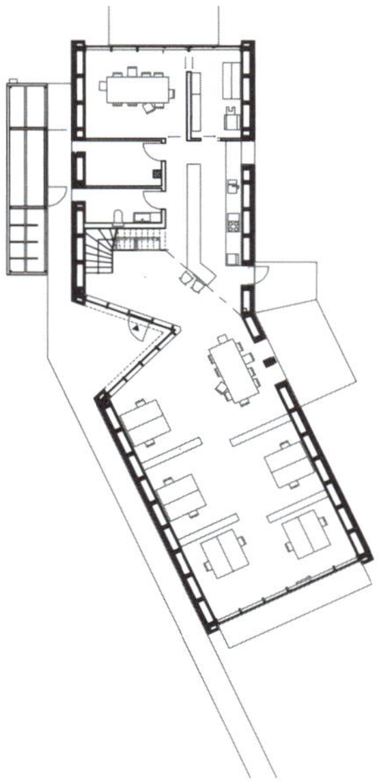

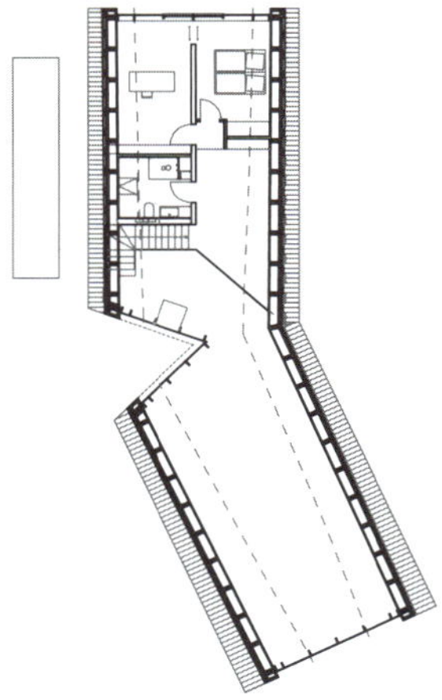

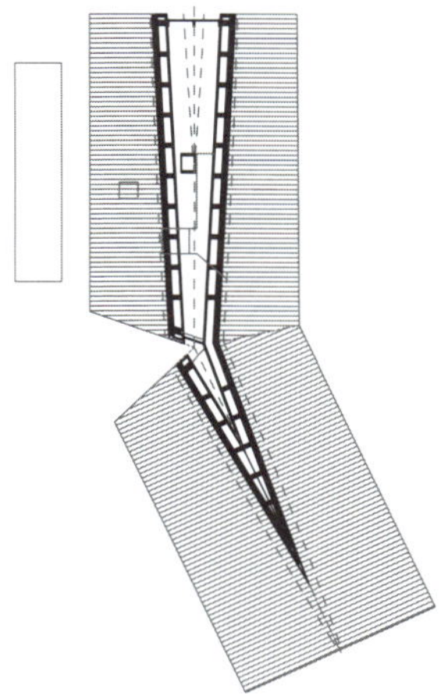

Architecture: asdfg Architekten and Jehann Gisli Brunk
Client: eff plan
Year of completion: 2016
No. of bedrooms: 3 rooms
Gross floor area: 320 m²
Wood: 550 m² of larch used for façade and roof, 610 m² of birch used for interior walls, furniture, stairs, railing and kitchen

Custom furniture and birch walls combined with polished concrete floors and countertops compliment the bright interior.

Future use and flexibility were a key consideration in the design. While the building currently functions as a small office with numerous homelike amenities, the design can easily be converted to a purely residential building.

Openings blur the boundaries between interior and exterior.

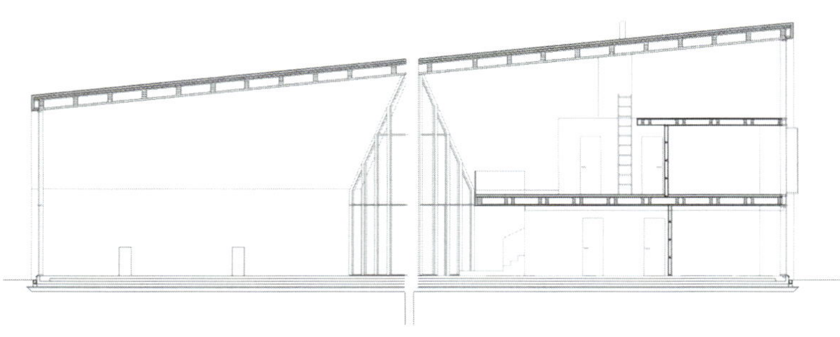

DOLUNAY VILLA
MUĞLA, TURKEY

Situated along the coast of the Aegean Sea in Turkey's south-western province of Muğla, the private Dolunay Villa has been carefully sited amid the natural rugged setting, prioritizing the spectacular sea views. Fascinated by the local landscape, they wanted it to flow through the interior spaces and effectively disguise the building. The design uses the natural contours of the site to create a low-rise building that appears as a single-story structure on approach. The main entrance takes you directly to the heart of the villa with the private family quarters to the eastern side with exceptional views of the setting sun over the Aegean. The journey through the villa is from opaque to open, reflecting the differing levels of privacy throughout and the design seeks to blur the boundaries between inside and outside living, with the large glass doors along the façade that slide back completely providing an unobstructed flow of space between the interior and exterior spaces. The house features a handcrafted undulating structural timber roof, designed in conjunction with Swiss firm Blumer Lehmann. The prefabricated and precision-engineered structure contains substantially less carbon than a typical concrete roof.

Architecture: Foster + Partners
Participating offices: Design Group Istanbul, Artiko architects
Client: Kaplankaya and Dolunay Villa
Year of completion: 2019
No. of bedrooms: 5 rooms
Gross floor area: 1,668 m²
Wood: 56 m³ of oak, 205.5 m³ of spruce, 15 m³ of beech

The villa merges with its surroundings by using material matching the site.

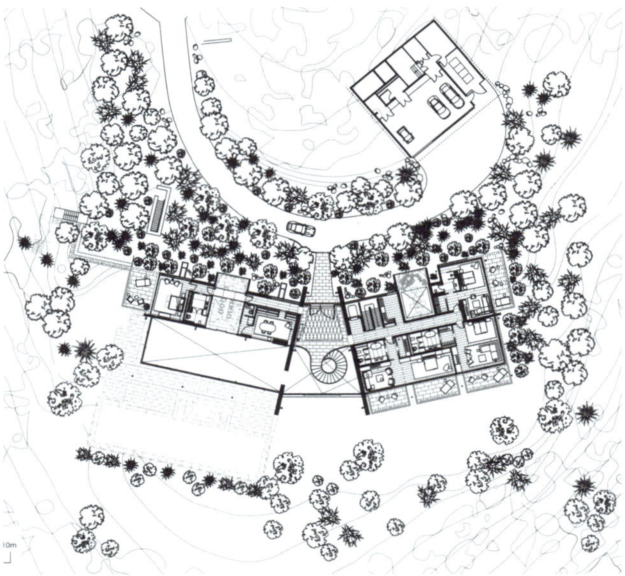

The central feature stair that connects the two levels is made from solid Portuguese limestone and is supported by post-tensioned cables running through the stone. The balustrades are made from thin glass tubes with a timber handrail that has been bent and shaped on site. There is a smaller sunset pavilion closer to the coast that features natural stone walls, olive groves, wooden tables and a bamboo soffit. Inspired by the villa's immediate surroundings, the natural interior material palette consists of stone, wood and bronze.

ICOARÉ HOUSE
OLIVEIRA DE AZEMÉIS, PORTUGAL

The site of the house has uneven terrain. The house was built to bridge that unevenness and seeks alignment with the neighboring buildings. An apparent structure of concrete walls connects the ground floor of the house to the site. It supports the steel structure, made in an industrial environment, of the first floor. The two materials contrast in strength and lightness: Concrete – subtlety and sensitivity – makes a connection to the land, while steel seeks very subtle proportions and clearly identifies the work of detail, of manpower, of locksmiths and carpenters.

Wood is used for the structure and coating of the exterior and interior walls. This house is considered a laboratory for the interaction of construction and design in various aspects. First, the test assembly and final assembly of the steel structure. Second, understand the difficulty in which the same concept can be brought to its maximum potential regarding the design and execution of the details. Third, aspects of the finishing were developed in an artisan way in joint work of architect and carpenter.

Architecture: Aste Arquitectura / Ana Isabel da Costa e Silva
Client: confidential
Year of completion: 2020
No. of bedrooms: 3 rooms
Gross floor area: 215 m²
Wood: African afzélia used for exterior cladding, interior floors and window frames, Portuguese pine used for light wood frame walls, Brazilian IP used for exterior deck

Further, there was a desire to use environmentally friendly materials and sustainable processes. The enormous difficulty of achieving this goal in Portugal becomes clear in a coherent way. More than half the materials used are environmental friendly, namely the option for a green roof, use of thermal insulation of black cork agglomerate and celluloses made from recycled paper, flooring with wood used from frames, reuse of rainwater for irrigation, and reforestation of the land.

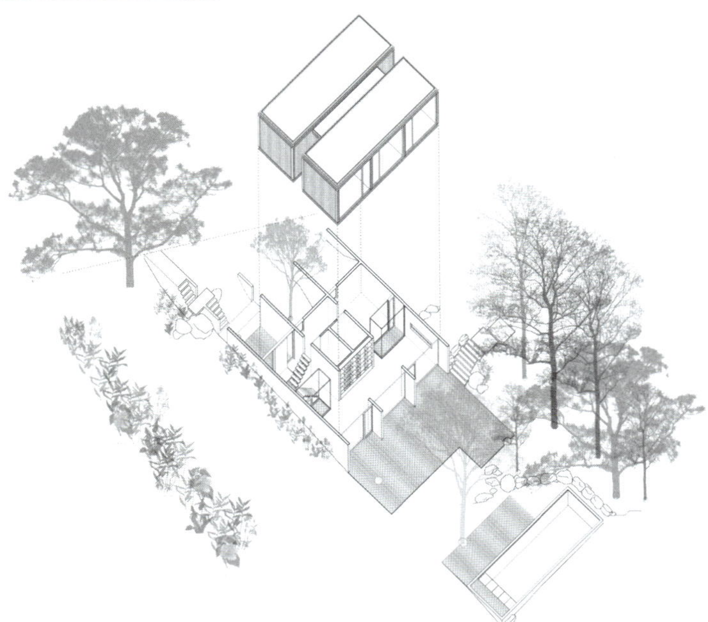

Principles of lightness and essentiality take shape in this design.

HOLIDAY HOME
GEMESES, PORTUGAL

This house was designed with the idea of family life in mind and as a vacation home and retreat for the whole family, including a younger generation. At the same time, the building was not only to stand for a long time but also to be built quickly. It was built in a teardrop-shaped triangle in a corner of Gemeses, in Esposende, towards the banks of the Cávado River. The design aligns with the classical conditions of architecture in the area, from the various commitments with the place to the dialogue between people and the rules established by public entities. The house has two floors to free up as much land as possible. Then a square floor plan was designed, using all the quadrants of the surrounding landscape, for example, for solar alignment or for the greater expanse of the forest, which disappears from view to the north. The house stands on a foundation of concrete. Here, 12-centimeter-thick wooden boards were laid horizontally and concreted from top to bottom.

A large social space for the whole family, both interior and exterior, and three units for an overnight stay, were built. The lower floor was to form an intermediate space between the outside and the inside. To the south, the interior solarium extends over a threshold to the outdoor terrace. Thanks to the large window the basement does not feel closed but is an open space that protects from the weather. The ground floor was reserved as a social space and includes, among other things, the living room and kitchen, but laundry and bathroom as well.

Architecture: Atelierdacosta
Client: Miguel Sousa Neves
Year of completion: 2019
No. of bedrooms: 3 rooms
Gross floor area: 280 m^2
Wood: 100 m^2 of lunawood / laminated pine beams used for external cladding and structure, 200 m^2 of birch plywood used for internal walls and window frames, 90 m^2 of ash wood used for flooring

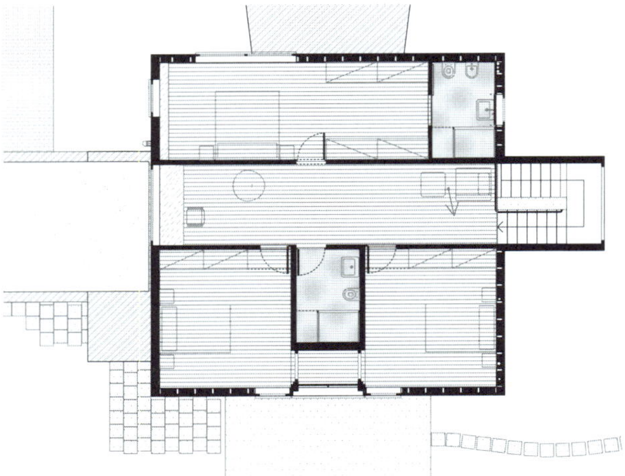

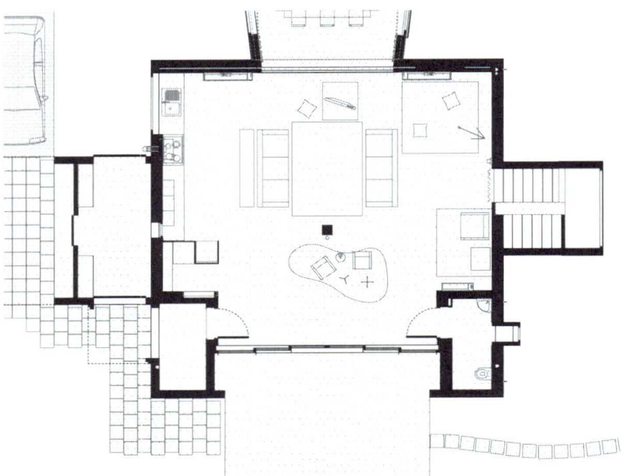

On the upper floor are the three bedrooms. Reached by stairs, there is a corridor that divides the whole building. This corridor is intentionally oversized so it can be used as an additional, recreational space or a more intimate workspace.

The aim was to build a family home for this, but also for following generations.

Architecture: ArchitekturWerkstatt
Client: Christian Leitner
Year of completion: 2019
No. of bedrooms: 3 rooms
Gross floor area: 403.82 m²
Wood: 1,247.5 m² of CLT spruce used for exterior walls and ceilings, 230 m² of wood fibers used for external insulation, 773.5 m² of massive oak used for interior paneling and suspended ceiling, 230 m² of larch used for façade and terrace

HOUSE LEEL
ELLMAU, AUSTRIA

The new building is the replacement for the residential part of the farm Huben in Ellmau. The owners wanted to build their new home, including a granny apartment and yoga studio, on the same site where they had already made their home thirty years ago. Matured in the decision that the new building should become a pure timber construction, it was important to them to use the place as optimally as possible. This means optimally capturing the fantastic view of the Wilder Kaiser, the existing tree population including the fruit trees, the adjacent barn for suckler cow husbandry and, above all, the sunlight over the course of the day and the year.

Parts of the existing building were thus reused and put to new use. A separation of the living areas of the parents, the owners' granny apartment and the yoga studio, was a prerequisite. The location of the parents on the upper floor as an independent unit required that an elevator was installed for accessibility. The studio is located on the ground floor, with a three-sided view, which has the advantage that there is no mutual interference between visitors and residents.

The implementation of solid wood construction, including thermal insulation made of wood fiber, wooden façades in the protected area made of larch, up to the continuous interior surfaces made of solid oak creating a unique atmosphere. The façade, which is directly exposed to the weather, is realized with solid-colored, dark fiber concrete panels.

The roof is covered with extensive greenery, so that this 'fifth façade' becomes part of the environment.

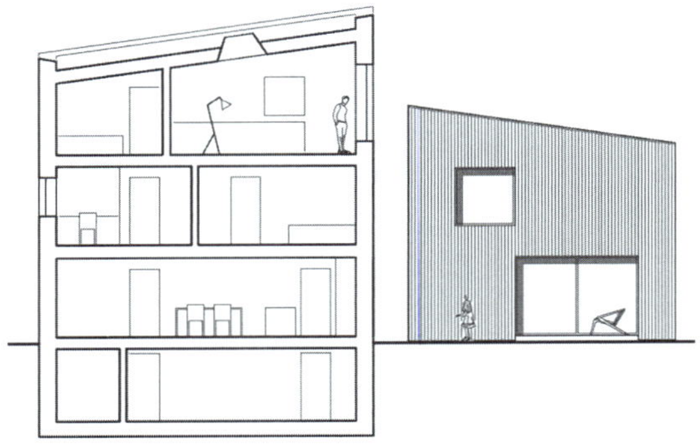

Architecture: Bayr Glatt Guimaraes Architekten
Client: confidential
Year of completion: 2021
No. of bedrooms: 4 rooms
Gross floor area: 304 m²
Wood: 450 m² of silver fir used for façade, 620 m² of various types of pine used for flooring, windows, stairs, doors and carpented furniture

HOUSE S
FRIEDBERG, GERMANY

The two structures form differentiated outdoor spaces due to their shifted arrangement on the triangular plot. Towards the street, a semi-public courtyard was created as a prelude and meeting point; towards the stream, two protected, private gardens were formed. With its flexible use, the small house complements the large house, which is designed as a compact, three-story residential building.

Due to the different uses as a residential house, apartment and practice, two structures were formed, which compensate for the limited space and the site layout by their height with two and three floors. Two space-saving, tower-like volumes were created, which are bounded above by a sloping roof surface. Due to the orientation to the busy street, adjoining rooms, the bathrocms and access areas are located on these sides of the buildings.

The living spaces and rooms are oriented to the garden side with large openings. In the large residential building, a spacious living and dining area with a kitchen is located on the first floor. A supplementary living and working area was placed in the attic to obtain the best view from the very top via large windows. From this light-flooded space, natural light falls throughout the house down to the first floor. At the lowest point in the attic is the bedroom, which gives a cozy and pared-down impression due to the low ceiling height and the restriction to the bed and a chest of drawers.

Multiple windows allow light to pass through both buildings entirely.

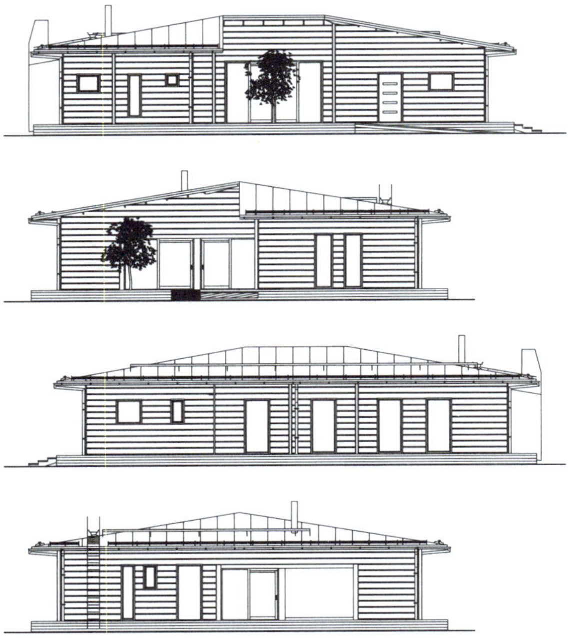

Architecture: KOAN Architecture / Marko Simsiö
Interior design: Maru Hautala
Landscape design: Asako Hashimoto
Client: Honkarakenne Ltd.
Year of completion: 2022
No. of bedrooms: 3 rooms
Gross floor area: 192 m²
Wood: spruce logs used for external load bearing walls, heat treated spruce used for the terraces

HONKA HAIKU NAANTALI, FINLAND

The Japan-inspired Honka Haiku is in harmony with the surrounding nature – the connection to nature, the naturalness of materials, and smart solutions for eco-friendly living provide the site with sustainable luxury.

Honka Haiku is the result of close collaboration between architect Marko Simsiö, interior designer Maru Hautala and landscape architect Asako Hashimoto. The architecturally interesting Nordic log house inspired by Japanese harmony has been fitted in the stunning archipelago plot in a way that respects the surrounding nature and protects the rocky terrain and pine forest.

The house forms around a sheltered atrium and the line between the outdoor and indoor spaces is in constant motion. The calming courtyard serves as an extension of the lounge and dining room, and it also blends into the conservatory and spa section. Everything is open and private at the same time.

A tree planted in the middle of the site creates a strong connection to nature.

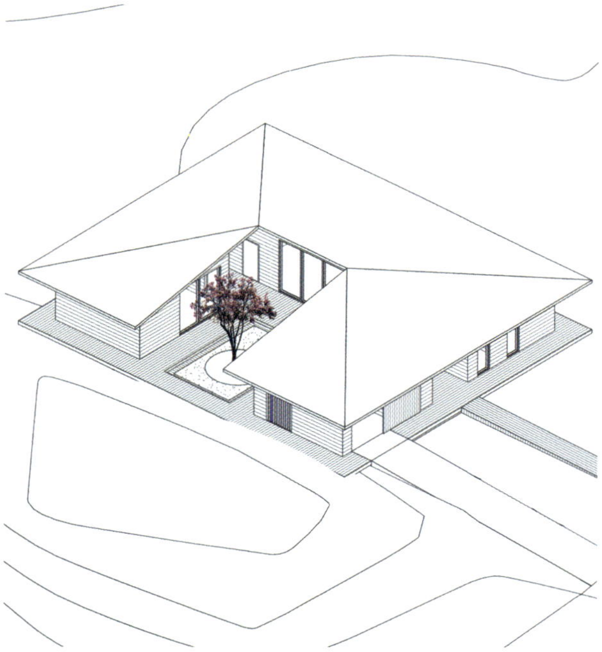

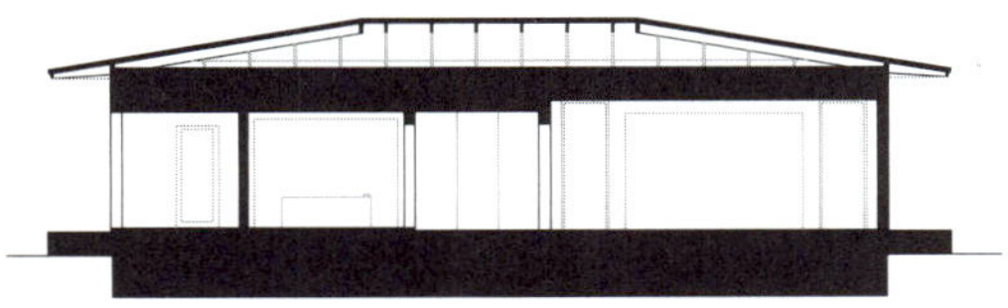

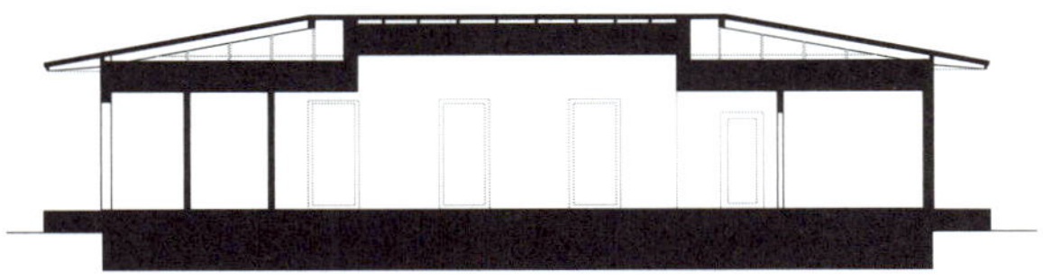

Honka Haiku is a trailblazer in sustainable and healthy living. The log house produces its own electricity and has achieved the best energy-efficiency rating A. With this Honkarakenne log house, one gets a holistic approach to keeping indoor air healthy as well as modern smart-home solutions designed to respond to everyday situations and the surrounding conditions. The technology blends in with the harmonious look of the log house.

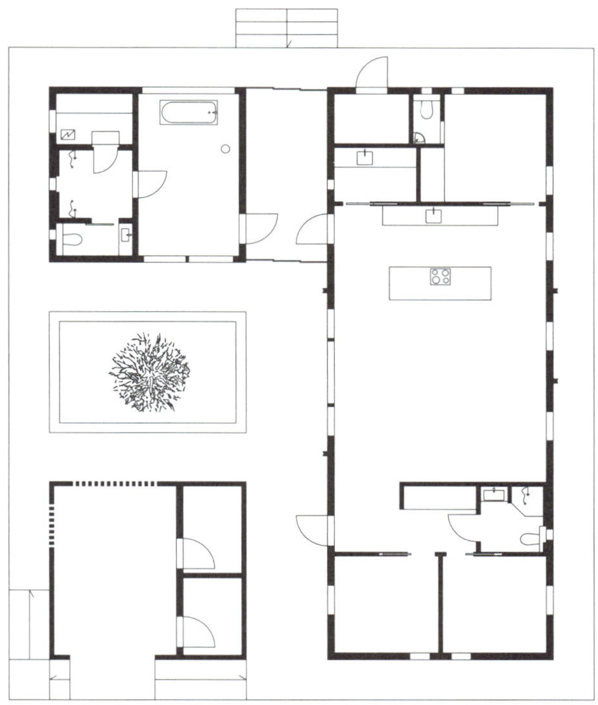

Peace and tranquility that is given to its inhabitant helps to maintain a balanced life.

LATHHOUSE
SAGAPONACK, NY, USA

The architectural context of Sagaponack, New York. is a unique mix of modernism, contemporary refinement, historicism, and rural farmland. Lathhouse reflects a purposeful agrarian context influenced by the region's local agricultural history and is conceptually inspired by the eponymous lath house. A traditional gabled farm structure made of wood laths or slats spaced to reduce sunlight while permitting ventilation. This wood detail is also found in corn cribs, drying barns, and livestock shelters.

The two-story gabled residence is oriented east-west and clad with a singular exterior material of weathered wood reclaimed from decades-old corral board snow fencing. The slatted screen provides privacy, limits exterior light emittance, and is used for solar shading. Operable glass walls open to a large terrace at the living room and a wood-slatted pergola at the kitchen. The pool house emulates the house with a pergola, sliding glass walls, and wood details.

The interior finishes are inspired by the light and shadow play of the slats over the glass walls and skylights. The clean design aesthetic, scale and detail of bespoke furniture pieces and custom-designed cabinetry reflect a depth of craft congruent with the architecture experience.

Architecture: Birdseye
Interior design: Brooke Michelsen Design
Landscape design: Wagner Hodgson Landscape Architecture
Client: confidential
Year of completion: 2020
No. of bedrooms: 5 rooms
Gross floor area: 470 m²
Wood: 1,728 m² of repurposed corral board used for exterior tongue and groove vertical siding, horizontal slats and vertical battens, 166 m² of ipe used for exterior decks, 535 m² of European white oak used for interior flooring and ceilings

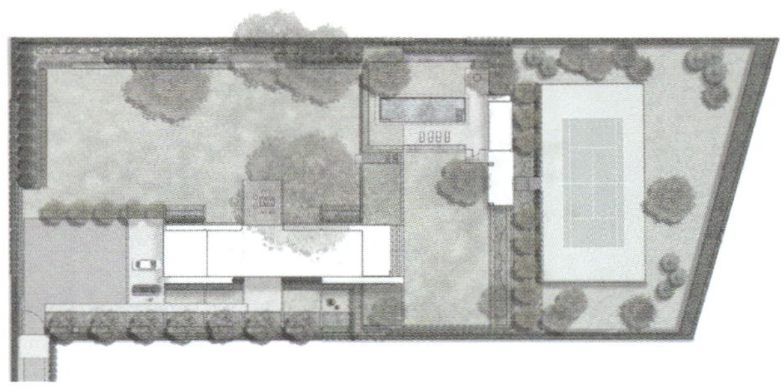

The interior pleasantly harmonizes with the exterior façade.

The repurposed wood, electrically based geothermal heating and cooling, closed cell insulation, mechanical fresh air system, and insulated windows all contribute to the efficiency of the design and sustainability of the house. A concealed gutter and downspout system collects and disperses water to dry wells to mitigate erosion on the site.

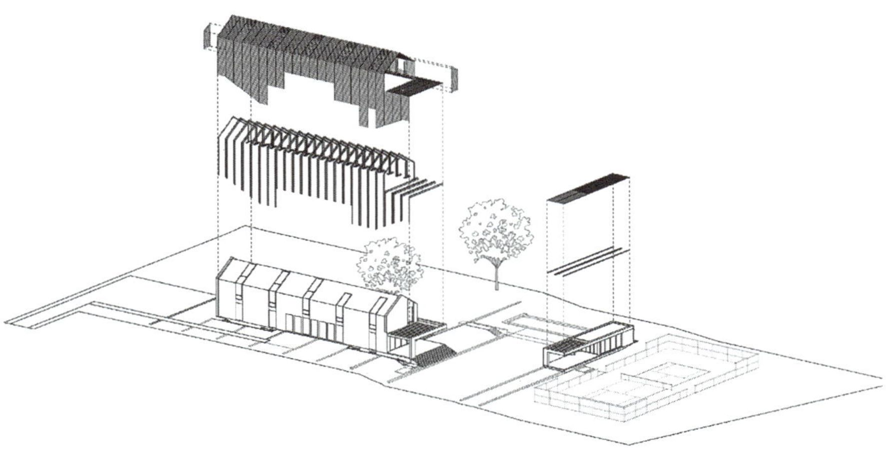

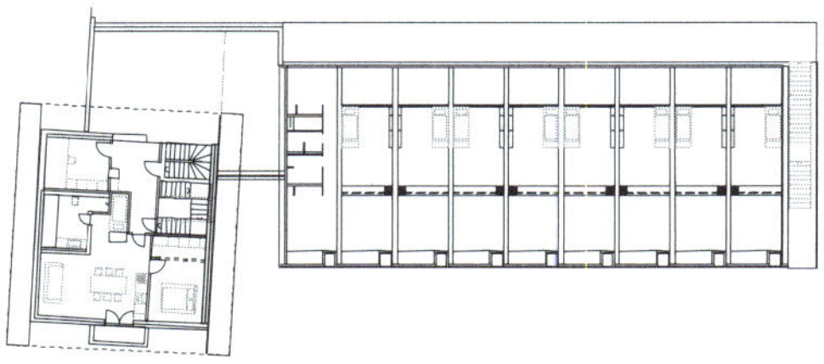

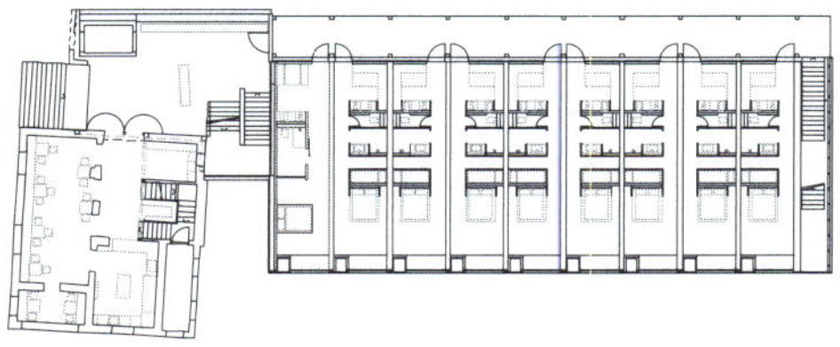

Architecture: Beer Bembé Dellinger
Client: VEHBL Baugemeinschaft GbR, gap.Quartiersen
Year of completion: 2017
No. of bedrooms: 3 to 5 rooms per house
Gross floor area: 7,500 m²
Wood: spruce used for interior, walls and roof, larch used for exterior

GARMISCH QUARTERS
GARMISCH-PARTENKIRCHEN, GERMANY

The project on Krankenhausstraße in Garmisch-Partenkirchen reuses an inner-city site and complements the surroundings with a new mix of utilizations. The urban redevelopment was carried out by a joint building venture. Four historic buildings were integrated into the new development. In the south, the closed hotel development provides structural noise protection from the busy streets of St. Martin-Straße.

On the property behind, rows of single-family homes and duplexes as well as multi-story apartment buildings form a screened, communally used green meadow that provides a view of the parish church and the foothills of the nearby mountain Kramerspitze. The reorganization of the area not only offered the opportunity to gradually develop a new, mixed-use neighborhood, but also the chance to receive, support and implement impulses and commitment from citizens of sustainable and future-oriented development of their town.

Following up on the projects claim “Old Garmisch lived anew” the Garmisch Quarters combine living with private work, creative workshops, an ice curling manufacturer and a hotel with a conference area and café. With the joint building venture, Baugemeinschaft in German, as the developer, the development as well as the mix of uses and density could be closely coordinated with residents and future user groups during the planning and construction process.

The houses create a mixed environment for business and recreational purposes.

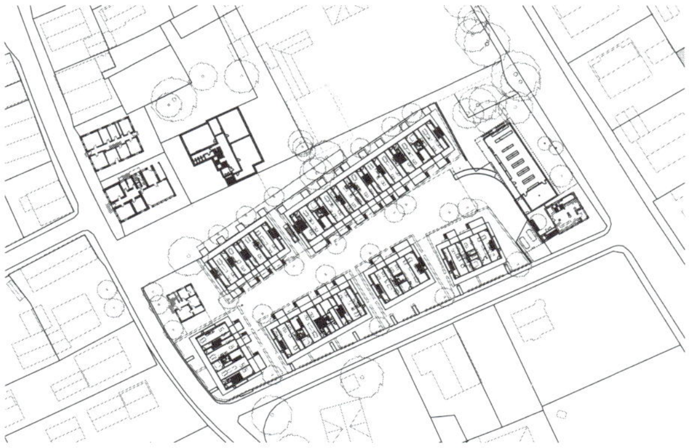

The functional requirements of the client are organized in a simple structure with a saddle roof, which is located according to the prominent topography and vegetation on the site. The traditional, regionally typical single courtyard, which historically joins all functions; living, storage, and working under one roof, serves as a content reference of the project. The single-story structure on the slope, which is visible from the southern access road, defines the right of way and arrival at the site and the interface between public and private.

On the first floor, in addition to the garage with storage space, are all public areas of the house with a generously open living/cooking/dining area and a checkroom with a day toilet. The open space, oriented north-west, directly connected to the kitchen, complements the uses and serves, due to the steep slope situation, as a garden substitute and protected open space. The two-story lighting gap facing south becomes a characteristic feature of the building due to its formulation in materiality and structure, and ensures appropriate light plays and distanced views into the building's interior.

FAMILY-HOME HERZGSELL
RADSTADT, AUSTRIA

Architecture: LP architektur
Client: Herzgsell Hans
Year of completion: 2020
No. of bedrooms: 2 rooms
Gross floor area: 290,15 m²
Wood: larch used for façade and majority of construction, spruce used for all of interior

Private areas as well as more intimate spatial zones with protected open spaces that cannot be seen are located in the basement and offer direct access to the garden. The affinity for the art of the client is taken into account with designated spaces for it. Aboveground, the building is designed as a constructive timber structure with an untreated, sawed larch façade or stamped concrete with natural stone inlays; belowground in-situ concrete is used.

Living, storage and work are united under a common roof.

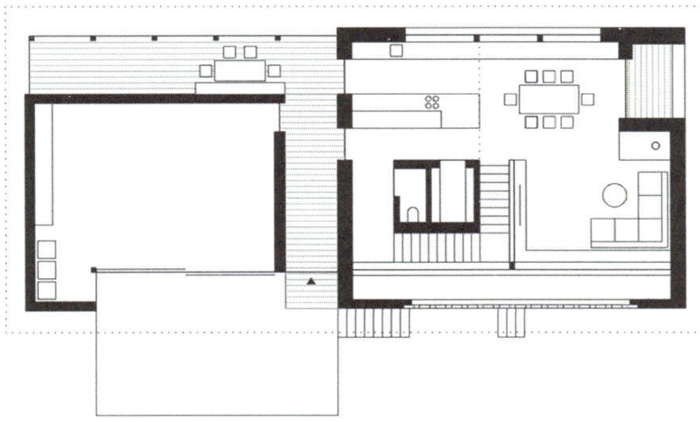

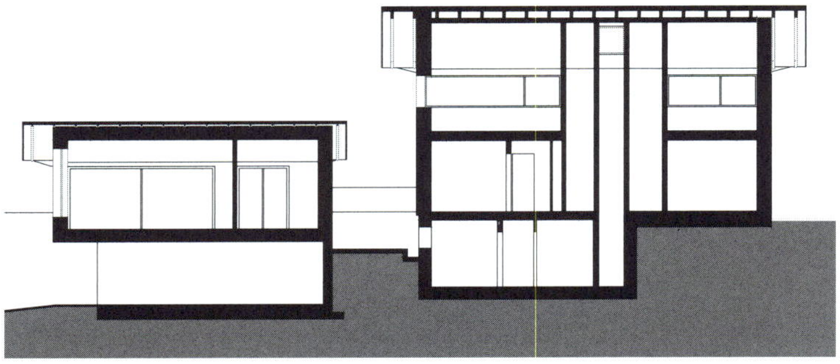

Architecture: CBA Clemens Bachmann Architekten and Lebensraum Holz
Client: confidential
Year of completion: 2020
No. of bedrooms: 3 rooms
Gross floor area: 250 m²
Wood: 43,8 m³ of different spruce types used for roofs, ceilings and walls, 1 m³ of larch used for walls

HOUSE N
SAMERBERG, GERMANY

This timber home is a custom build project for a married couple from Munich. The job was to build a main house as well as an outbuilding that can be rented out as a vacation home. The main house is centered around a large gallery in which the staircase is placed. All rooms are arranged around that centerpiece.

In the concept, themes such as widening and narrowing, insight and outlook, as well as light and shadow were taken up. The scheme of materials and colors was reduced to white walls, black painted timber and natural oiled wooden flooring and details. The large-scale glazing provides impressive views of the surrounding mountains of the Chiemgau foothill that contribute to the theme of light and shadow and link the inside to the outside. While in the public rooms, like the dining area downstairs, the windows reach from the floor to the top on the upper floor, the windows do not reach all the way to the floor to create more privacy. To translate the open space of the large-scale windows downstairs, the windows on the upper floor are arranged across the corner to enable a panoramic view of the nearby mountains.

The dark wooden façade contrasts with the surrounding buildings and yet blends into the local landscape thanks to the simple arrangement of the windows. It gives the house a calm and modest atmosphere and contributes to the overall modern and elegant look of the building. The project was planned with the company Lebensraum Holz. The house is energy-efficient and built in a post and beam construction. The two volumes fit into the topography of the site and create a contained garden space facing the street.

Themes such as widening and narrowing, insight and outlook, as well as light and shadow are at the center of this build.

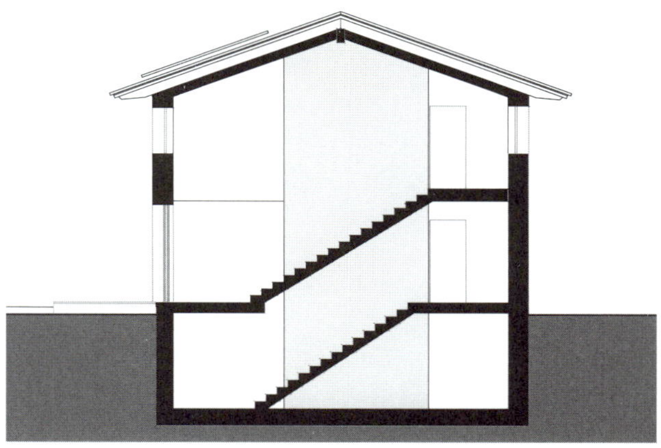

HOUSE IN SAMAMBAIA
PETRÓPOLIS-RJ, BRAZIL

The house was projected and built by Rodrigo Simão for himself and his family, preserving relief, stones and native trees, creating functional spaces that integrate domestic life with the nature of the place. The entrance of the house is a deck of wooden planks. The steel structure used most in the building made it possible to have large spans, allowing large windows and a view of the beautiful landscape of the region. Most of the house has flooring made of polished concrete slabs. The concrete is also exposed in walls and slabs, molded in the formwork with battens, thus exploiting its properties.

The stairs to the mezzanine and terraces are made of profiles of recycled steel and pink peroba planks. Doors made of solid hardwood, ladders made of hardwood, covers with wooden floors, countertops for the bathroom, wooden furniture and yellow light fixtures made exclusively for the project give the building a sense of domesticity. The lightweight structural set of the house rests on masonry stone walls that compose the foundation by lifting it off the floor to avoid moisture and animals, contributing to the lightness of the structure.

Architecture: Rodrigo Simão Arquitetura
Carpentry: Nilton Pica Pau, Luis Carlos Valadares
Client: confidential
Year of completion: 2017
No. of bedrooms: 4 rooms
Gross floor area: 375 m²
Wood: 125 m² of various reclaimed wood used for façade cladding and entrance deck, 260 m² of ipe used for roof support

The curved roof tilts in the direction of the rising sun, allowing light to pass at all times.

The stones were reclaimed from a hundred year old wall and implemented by a local craftsman. The planting was done by the residents, trying to incorporate native species. The house received additional outdoor spaces, such as a playroom and an art studio for the architect's wife, complementing the architecture and landscape design. The concepts of open space, use of materials in their natural form and integration with nature are intended to inspire the family to simplicity and a functional and integrated lifestyle.

The entrance space doubles as an outdoor living room.

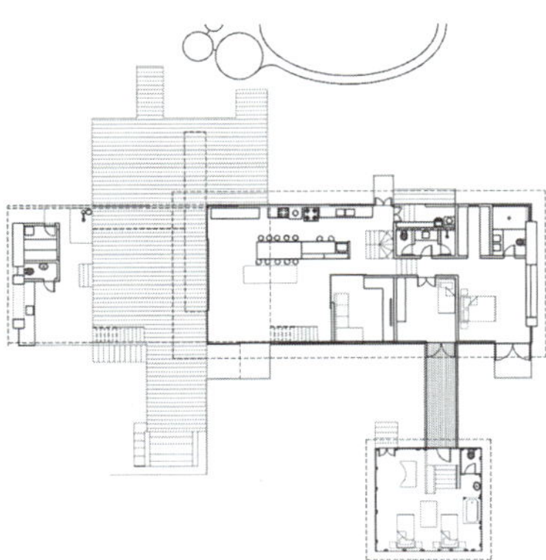

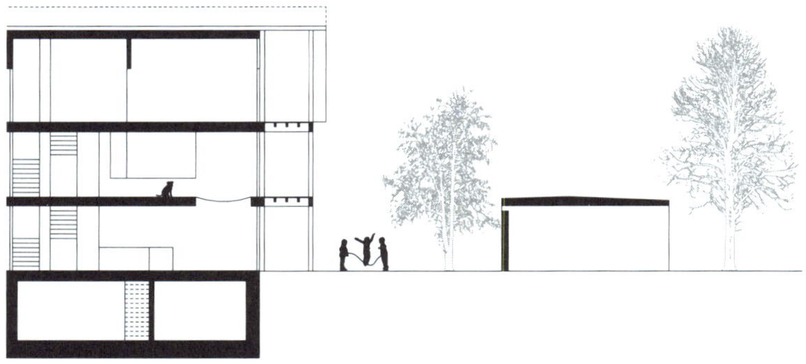

Architecture: dunkelschwarz
Client: confidential
Year of completion: 2021
No. of bedrooms: 3 rooms
Gross floor area: 417.03 m²
Wood: silver fir used for solid timber construction and furniture, larch used for rear ventilated façade, ash used for floors

HOUSE L
ELSBETHEN, AUSTRIA

Effortlessness, privacy, an open and bright atmosphere as well as a flowing transition between inside and outside were the wishes laid out by the owners.

The clients wanted a house with an outbuilding and canopied entrance. The building has a shielding courtyard towards the bypassing street, providing both privacy and flow. Through terraces and balconies, the entire living space is enabled to engage with this secure but open area, also creating a connection to the south side garden. While the rectangular floor plan and steep gable roof align with the surrounding houses, the inside formulates a rather unconventional use of open space using nets spanning the living area. The bright and soft-looking ash wood installed by Fisher Parkett spans throughout the house adding to the light nature of the building.

Comfort and warmth is the primary focus of this resident building.

The flowing spacial figure across floors builds the center of the family home by linking kitchen, fireplace, dining area and diwan and simultaneously creating the unique character of the house – a home for daily use that offers coziness and support, implemented by carpenters Innovaholz and Tischlerei Speigner. The overall architectural concept can be seen as an approval of daily life rather than a stiff and inflexible construction.

KUKU-RANNA KINETIC
VÄÄNA-JÕESUU, ESTONIA

The summer house in Vääna-Jõesuu is like the archetype of a tepee or the steep slope of a farmhouse roof in the middle of nature. The minimalist, tent-like form often used in the region's cottage architecture in the 1970s has been complemented by kinetic elements, turning the laconic volume into a contemporary light and airy summer house.

When not used, the house with no permanent residents remains closed and unnoticed. The wooden façade is given a yakisugi finish, the side elevations have a marked char texture while the charred layer on the sloping surfaces has been partly washed away and thus is grayish in color. This way the house blends in with the surrounding pine tree trunks. As the residents arrive, the shutters rise up as wings revealing a large glass wall on the main façade leading to a living area in light hues. The open shutter will form a roof over the terrace in front of the living room. The glass wall below the shutter opens only halfway, thus allowing the terrace and the interior to form a comprehensive whole.

When open, the roof provides shelter from rain and sunlight and when closed, it forms a practical storage space for garden furniture, while also shielding the interior from the street. The old double bass has now become a shelf. The otherwise gentle summer house does have its whims – it's a good idea to keep the fingers off as both the cladding with yakisugi finishing and the Corten steel can stain.

Architecture: Arhitektuuribüroo Eek & Mutso / Madis Eek
Engineering: Toomas Tammerik
Landscape design: Margit Mutso
Client: confidential
Year of completion: 2020
No. of bedrooms: 2 rooms
Gross floor area: 80 m²
Wood: 248 m² of burned wood yakisugi used for exterior façades and roof, 235 m² of waxed fir tree used for interior

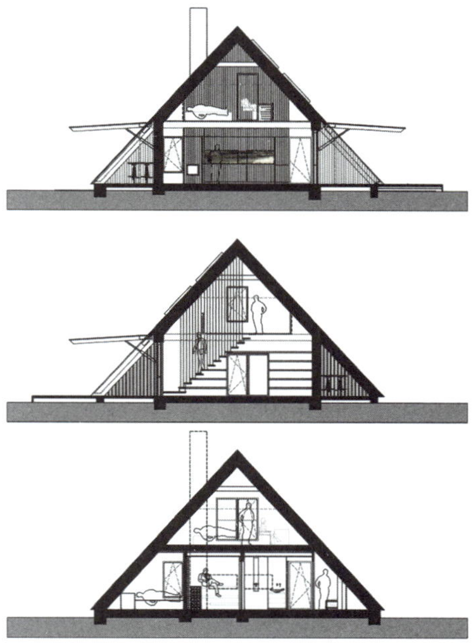

The oval window is recovered from a villa designed by Armas Lindgren.

There are also small surprises in the interior design with references to the surrounding nature and old traditions while leaving sufficient space for modern design and works of art by friends. The house stands on a concrete slab while the entire construction is timber. Also the exterior and interior finishing is wood while the construction of the shutters is steel ensuring the rigidity of the moving elements and the stability of the house.

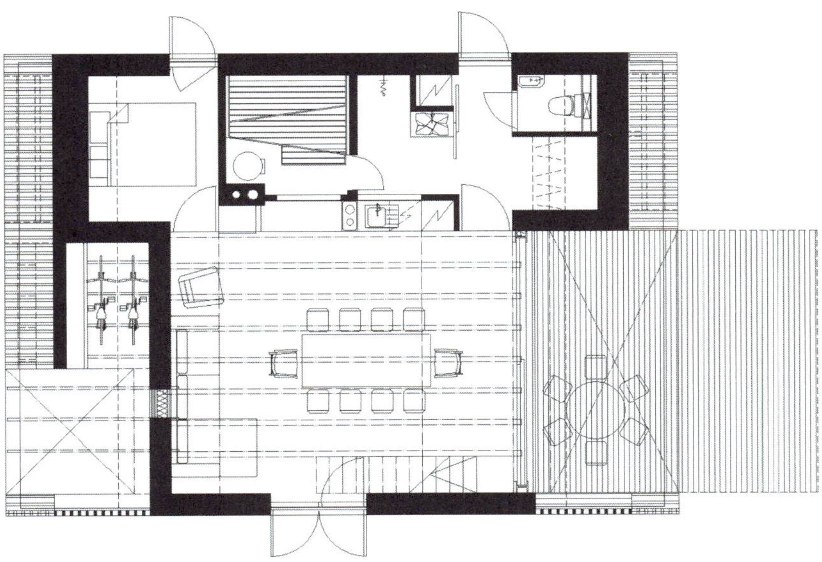

HOUSE VV
WÖRTH AM MAIN, GERMANY

Great importance was laid on an unadulterated material language of House VV. Façades made of natural larch cover the entire shape of the house. The protrusions of the roof as well as the window sill are kept as small as possible to ensure the natural graying of the wooden façade. The façade is ventilated and screwed in a concealed way. Few windows break through the envelope. The front door is part of the façade and merges with it. A change of material has not been carried out, because it would have been unnecessary. All façade elements and wooden details are carried out in larch.

Towards the garden, on the other hand, generous floor-to-ceiling panoramic sliding doors ensure maximum openness. Interior and exterior are connected and transitions are fluid. Whether starlight or rainy mood, nature lets its changing light colors flow into the room. The house is heated by a geothermal heat pump and there is a central ventilation system with heat recovery. A photo-voltaic system supplies the building with electricity.

Architecture: grams.grams architektur
Client: grams.grams architektur
Year of completion: 2020
No. of bedrooms: 3 rooms
Gross floor area: 180 m²
Wood: 205 m² of natural larch used for façade and terrace

The ground floor slab is a concrete core-activated foundation slab that was smoothed to its finished state as it set and the exposed concrete is only sealed. A steel and wooden staircase leads to the upper floor to the bedrooms, where parquet flooring was laid and the flooring was consistently in all rooms of the upper floor. This flooring was consistent applied in all rooms on the upper floor, including the bathroom.

A house defined by a simple, straight-forward design.

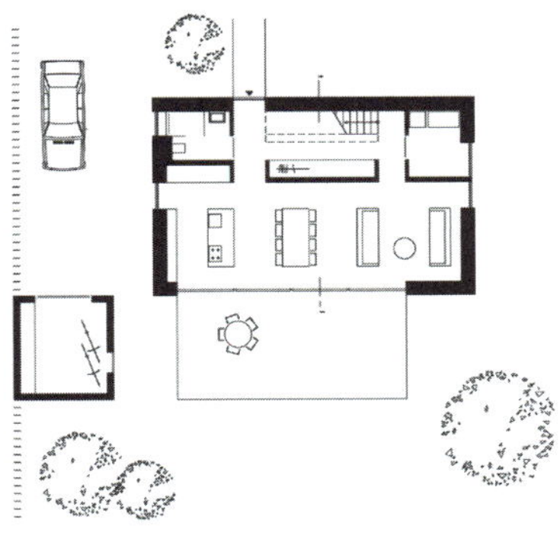

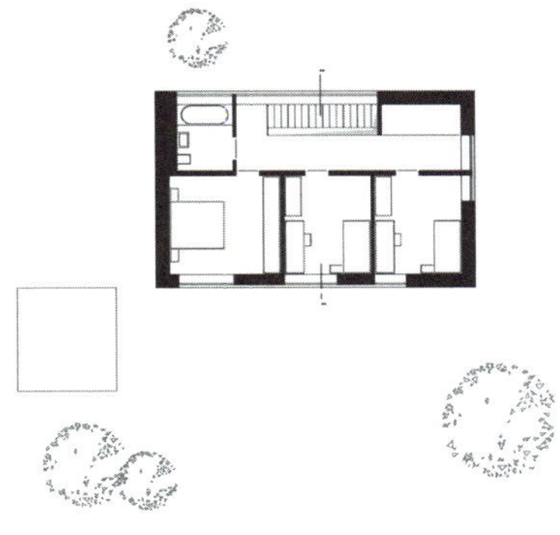

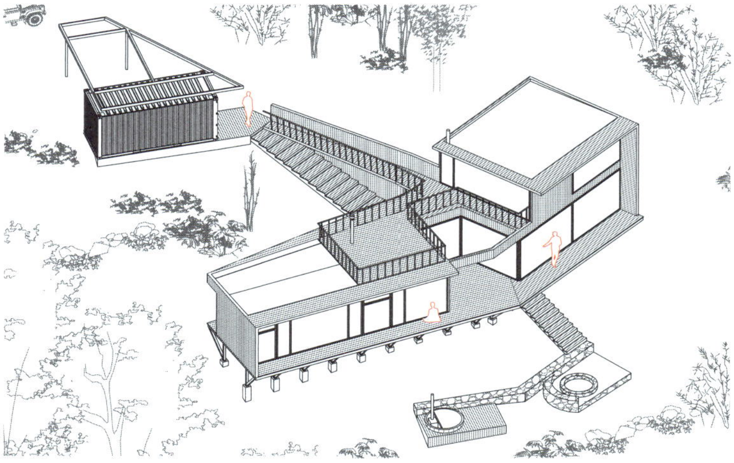

Architecture: nicolásCRUZarquitectos
Client: confidential
Year of completion: 2021
No. of bedrooms: 3 rooms
Gross floor area: 120 m²
Wood: 283,4 m² of radiata pine used for interior coverings, 312,6 m² of radiata pine used for structure and exterior coverings, poplar used for interior

S HOUSE
ALTO CENTINELA, CHILE

The land, located in a private subdivision in the hills of the Pupuya locality, is characterized by being long and thin. The lot is a steep slope that falls 85 meters to the east, from the interior circulation of the subdivision towards a ravine dominated by native forests. Given the topography, different views of the landscape are possible; distant views of the fields with the Andes mountain range and to the Rapel River. The house is located as far away as possible from the internal street, right at the point where the steepest slope begins. In this way, the proposal uses the full available width of the land, generating a turn, in the manner of a fan, seeking to obtain a panoramic view of the landscape.

The building is structured by means of four platforms and two volumes. The first; from which one can access the upper terrace platform or the intermediate platform. From this spot, one goes down to the lower platform of outdoor recreation programs. One walks downwards with access dominated by a terrace and views of the landscape, to the north, the first volume, with greater air, height and a variety of views, contains the main living room, dining room and kitchen, in addition to a mezzanine as a home office or guest bedroom, which opens onto a roof terrace.

The platform elevation allows for a broad view.

There is a space of private rooms, two bedrooms and two bathrooms with views to the east. A terrace roof constitutes the highest platform. The platforms and volumes are structured by means of a series of iron structure frames every one and a half meters, repeating and varying to generate the different platforms and volumes. These frames are filled with partition walls and wooden beams. On the outside, the buildings are covered with dyed black pine pood. Inside, the walls, doors and ceilings are covered with pine and poplar wood.

Wood dominates the space with its warm tones.

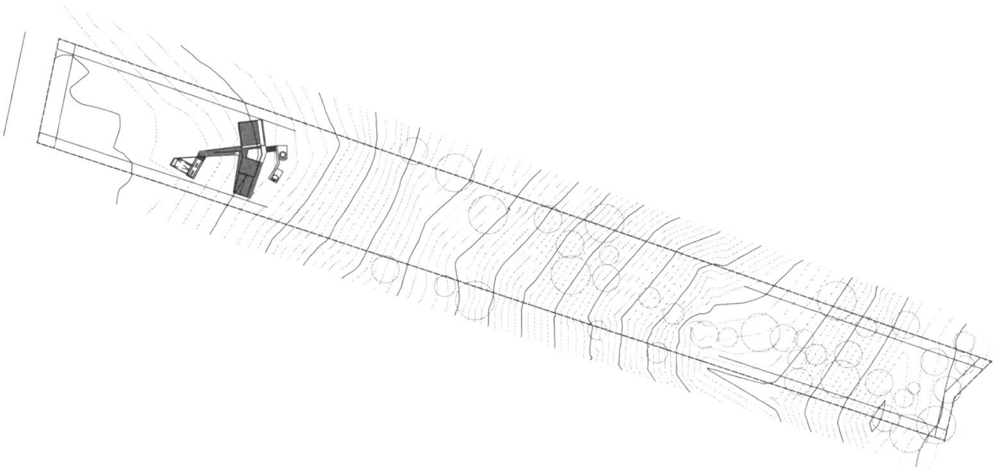

VILLAGE CENTER
ESCHENBACH, SWITZERLAND

With this project, the clients wanted to make room for the next generation. A space on the property occupied by a beloved shed was to be stylishly repurposed with a residence while maintaining the charm of the lovingly established garden. From the very beginning, the garden design had to be considered as important as the construction of the residential house to be planned. Without a doubt, only wood came into question for the choice of materials. Küng Holzbau knew how to turn the heartfelt wishes of the customer couple into reality.

The spacious veranda creates a semi-open space for family gatherings and social interaction. With its earth-toned design it almost gives a Mediterranian touch to the building.

Architecture: Matter Architekten
Participating offices: Küng Holzbau
Client: confidential
Year of completion: 2019
No. of bedrooms: 8 rooms
Gross floor area: 342 m²
Wood: 250 m³ of spruce used for construction, 410 m² of spruce used for façade, 400 m² of oiled oak used for flooring and furniture

The unglued wooden construction of the house, the style-defining archways of the gazebo and the harmonious use of materials and colors allow for a living atmosphere far removed from what one would normally expect from a new building. Ingenious and exciting details pepper the apartment building, about whose construction there would be many more stories to tell..

A heart-based project in the middle of town.

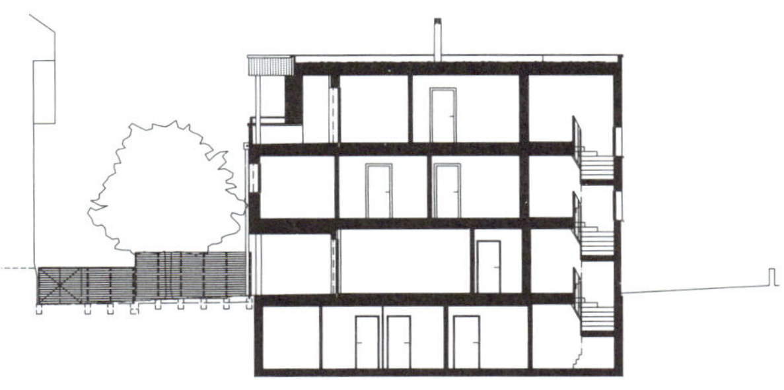

NODA HOUSE
NODA-SHI, JAPAN

This building is located in a newly developed residential area in the Mizuki suburb of Noda City in Chiba Prefecture, where the population density is very low. The architects were first struck by the rural quality of the area, no doubt an echo of its past, as there is an idyllic atmosphere in the air despite its location in the suburbs of Greater Tokyo.

In designing Noda House, the architects focused mainly on two things. The first was to design a plan for building houses that fit perfectly in this area. This house is a prototype of for-sale units, and the idea was to build houses with the same concept but with different floor plans in rapid succession once this prototype was completed.

Initially, they opted for a simple, single-story structure to meet economic rationality. Then the interior was equipped with several wooden boxes. The wooden box allows natural light into the living room and also serves as a staircase to access the roof terrace. Similar units will be strung together to form a row of houses and the wooden boxes add dynamism by creating a three-dimensional quality.

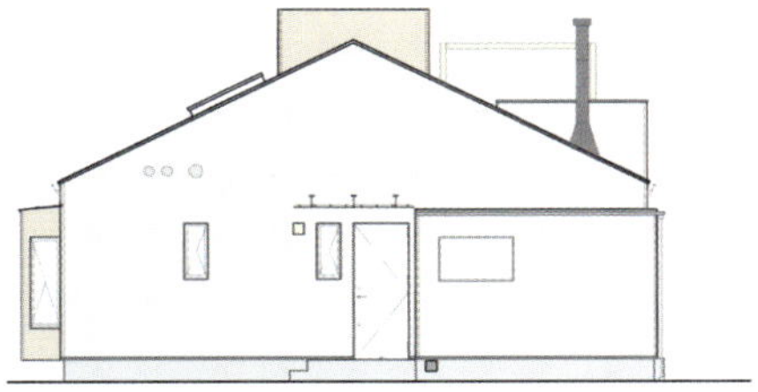

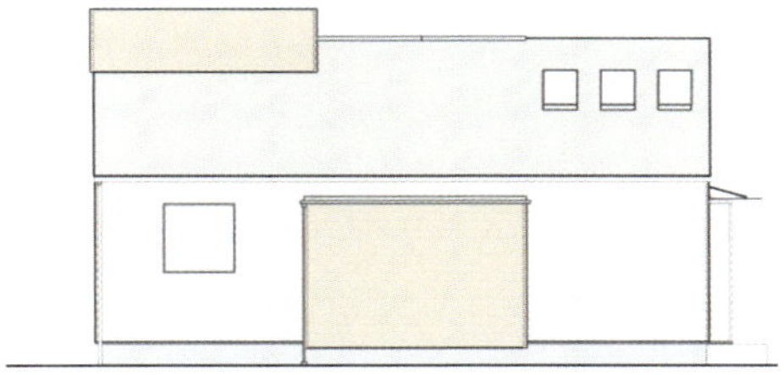

Architecture: HOAP
Design cooperation: Erika Okamoto
Client: confidential
Year of completion: 2017
No. of bedrooms: 2
Gross floor area: 113 m^2
Wood: 29 m^2 of red cedar used for the exterior wall, 76 m^2 of European oak used for interior flooring

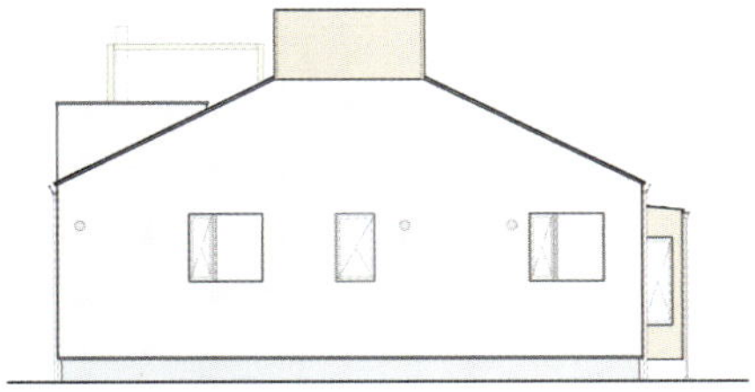

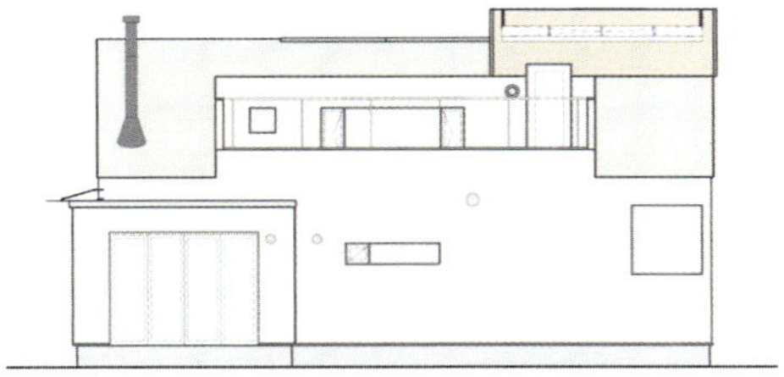

The second point was the attempt to revive a space for production within the house. In the past, houses had production-oriented spaces, such as first floor areas and barns. These spaces supported agricultural and production-oriented work such as making and repairing items. The architects reserved the space from the entrance to the first floor , to be alternatively used for different purposes. The walls are covered with lauan plywood to allow for more rustic uses such as handcrafted ornaments. The design also envisions that this space can be converted into a second living room by installing a charcoal stove.

This simple wooden home was created thinking outside the box.

GUEST HOUSE 3.0
SOSNIVKA, UKRAINE

Guest houses 3.0 are the new type of hotel rooms in the hotel and recreational complex Verholy Relax Park. Having a cozy patio allows the guests even more privacy along with nature. Only the forest, the noise of trees, the singing of birds and nobody else on the horizon.

This new type of guest house is maximally integrated into the surrounding pine forest thanks to the patio and the increased area of fully panoramic glazing. The houses are built from lightweight metal frame structures, made in accordance with the designers' drafts. Instead of the usual solid base, the house stands on a so-called screw base. This technology allows setting the structure quickly in any landscape – in this case among the pines without damaging any trees or their root system. So these houses are standing at least a meter above the ground.

Architecture: YOD Group
Client: Verholy Relax Park
Year of completion: 2019
No. of bedrooms: 1 room
Gross floor area: 80 m²
Wood: heat-treated alder for façades, veneered oak plywood used for walls, larch plates used for ceilings and terrace

Dark wood dominates the interior, making lights even more effective.

From outside buildings are covered with heat-treated plates made of solid alder. The interior floors are tiled and equipped with water heating; the walls are covered with plywood from veneered oak, ceilings and terrace – with larch plates. For finishing the architects used natural materials and natural color gamma.

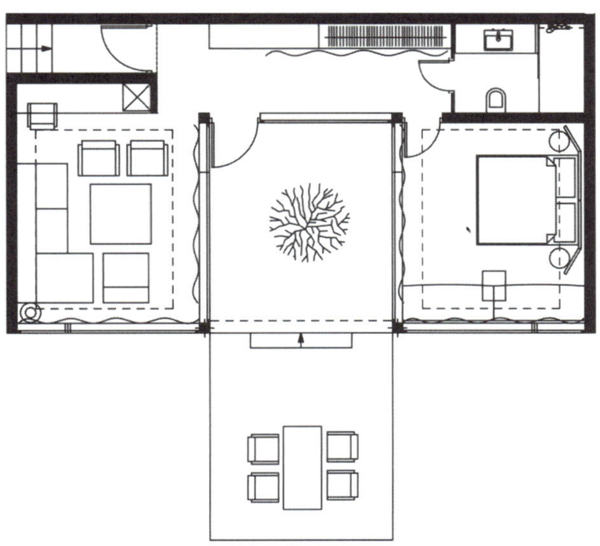

OPEN HOUSE
WARSAW, POLAND

Located near Warsaw, the building was designed for a young family who dreamed of a house in a modern barn style. The Open House is located on a narrow site, which naturally influenced the similar proportions of the building's plan. The shape of the elongated rectangle allowed for the appearance of the garden along the house, but the main garden is located in front of the building, which has been moved to the back of the site.

As a result, the glazed front elevation does not deprive the residents of intimacy but invites the garden inside. The Open House is perfect for a bookworm who dreams of hiding in the evening with a book but remains close to nature and the sunset. The floors are divided into a day and a night zone, but they are connected by a two-story living room and a mezzanine, allowing one to enjoy the view of the garden also from the first floor. An additional terrace, adjacent to the building from its southern side, stays an integral part of the entire building. The terrace can be accessed from the kitchen and living room and has been connected to the western terrace through an exit from the living room. The passage between the terraces — a break in the outer wall — provides southern light to the living area of the building.

Architecture: Z3Z Architekci
Client: confidential
Year of completion: 2019
No. of bedrooms: 3 rooms
Gross floor area: 200 m²
Wood: 200 m² of Siberian larch used for façade and terrace
4.5 m³ of pine used for roof construcion

It looks elegant and modern in any lighting condition.

A cozy house that lets its inhabitants connect to nature.

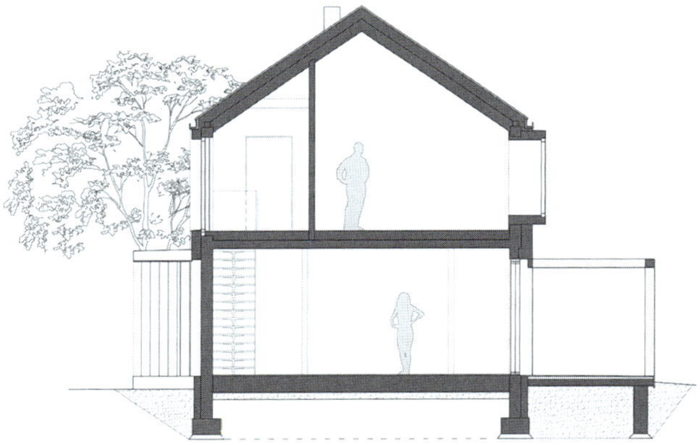

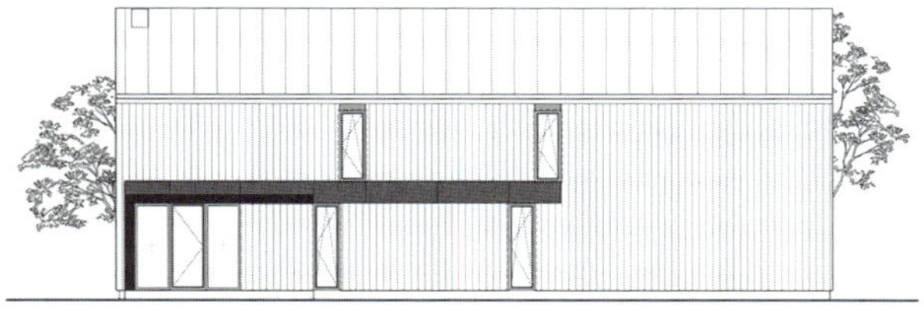

The building has a comfortable arrangement of rooms. The day zone has been divided into a storage part with an entrance and utility rooms, and a large open space accommodating a living room with fireplace, dining room and an open kitchen. The night zone on the first floor has been divided into children's rooms facing south, and the master bedroom with dressing room and loggia facing east.

HOUSE TNY55
INGELHEIM AM RHEIN, GERMANY

This sustainable, sufficient and cost-effective residential house in German KfW55 energy standard was planned for a family of four. For an excellent energy balance and a positive indoor climate, solid wood was chosen as an essential component of the house, which was complemented by ecological softwood fiber insulation. Not only over 53 tons of CO_2 were bound with this construction method, but also seven percent less area was used due to the filigree ten-centimeter thick walls. Inside, the surfaces of the prefabricated cross-laminated timber elements were finished in visible quality, so that the typical character of the spruce wood is preserved and further layers of plasterboard and plaster could be dispensed with. The design is based on functionality and efficient use of space in the smallest area and the highest quality of space. In order to plan the rooms sufficiently, the space requirements were precisely matched to the needs of the users and their usage behavior. The simple floor plan results from the clear south-west orientation of the residential house to the open garden. The spacious living area is entered via a buffer zone, with the guest toilet, storage space and access to the garage.

Architecture: Marc Flick Architekt
Client: confidential
Year of completion: 2021
No. of bedrooms: 3 rooms
Gross floor area: 165 m^2
Wood: 53 m^3 of spruce used for supporting structures, wall support and floors, wood fiber used for insulation, larch used for windows, doors and garage gate

The room-wide glazing allows the space to merge with the garden, extending it to the terrace if needed. The open staircase leads to the compact and clearly structured upper floor, which is divided into three rooms and the main bathroom. Except for the exterior plaster, composite materials were largely avoided; the house can be disassembled and recycled in individual parts. In addition to the solid wood walls, the interior roof clad with clay panels also contributes to a pleasant living climate with optimal humidity.

Large windows allow an almost panoramic view.

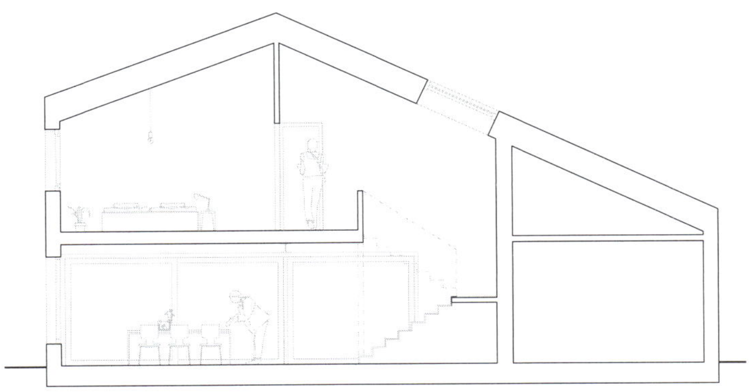

Tahoe Cabin is a vacation home located on the edge of South Lake Tahoe, a destination frequented by visitors near and far. Situated in a heavily wooded area, the design of the cabin avoids traditional design approaches in urban areas. In favor of preserving the natural environment, the site was under the local zoning code requiring a special permit when logging trees. By celebrating the constraint, the trees on site began to inform the design concept of this project while reinventing an architectural typology for a cabin in the forest.

A unique setback line, typically designated by the road in urban areas, began to be established by eleven pine trees on the site for this project while consciously avoiding clear-cutting the site for architecture. This created and defined a new buildable area and started to shape the form and space of the cabin, echoing to the existing trail path on site between trees. While volumetrically open, the requested programs were laid out in a sequential fashion from public function to a private function, from the entrance to the bedroom.

TAHOE CABIN
SOUTH LAKE TAHOE, CA, USA

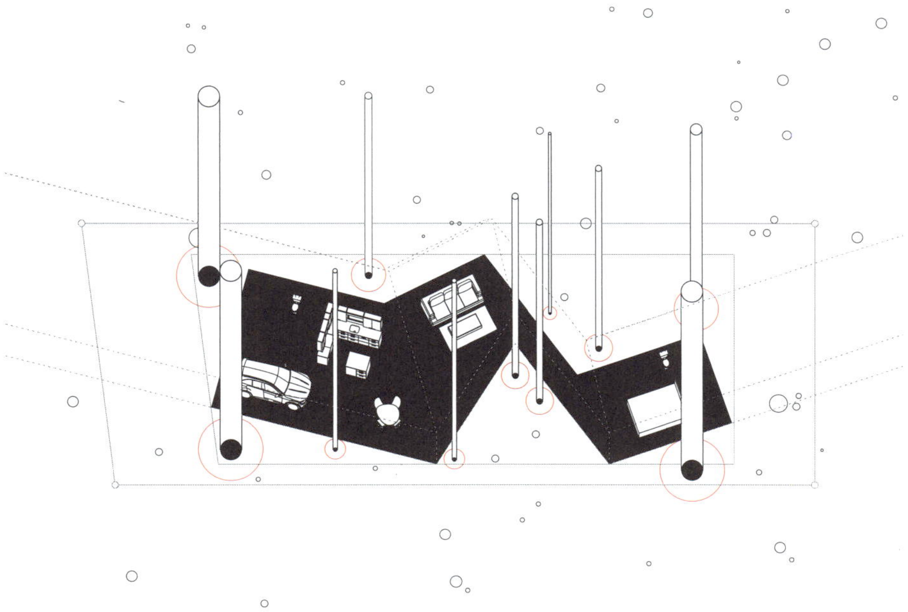

Architecture: Joongwon Architects
Client: confidential
Year of completion: 2019
No. of bedrooms: 2
Gross floor area: 215 m²
Wood: Siberian larch used for exterior siding, birch plywood used for interior finishes, birch used for flooring

The wooden cabin finds its way through existing trees.

The interior design of this project is finished with two materials: birch plywood for the ceiling, and white gypsum board walls in order to celebrate volumetric spaces. All the utilitarian elements such as lighting, electricity, furniture and storage were accommodated in the white wall to pursue a simple yet practical design.

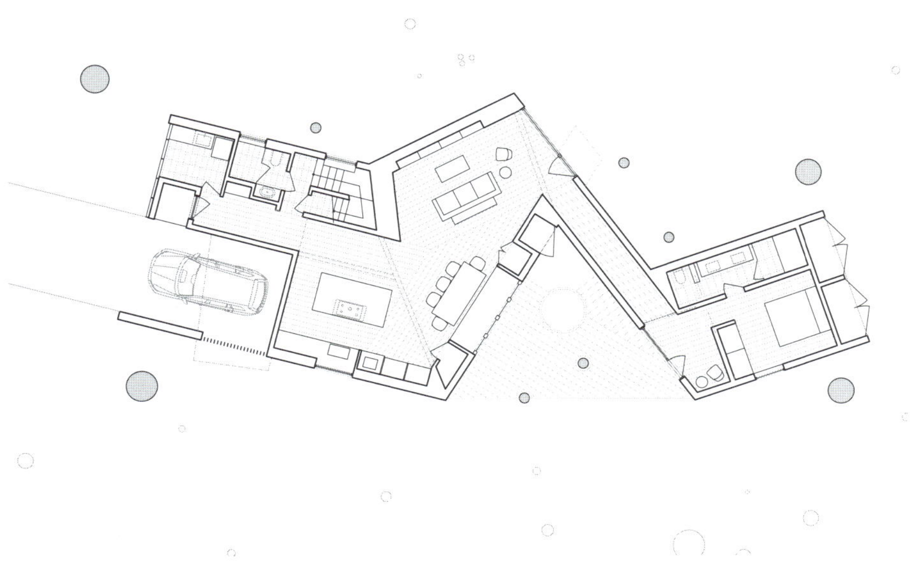

PH 56 is a maisonette penthouse with spectacular views of the surrounding landscape from a height of over forty meters. The lower level houses the kitchen, dining and living areas as well as the large main terrace. The consistent materiality with brushed oak, dark surfaces in ceramics, lacquer and spatula techniques create a calm, serene and at the same time introverted atmosphere. The kitchen is part of the overall concept. Filigree textured porcelain stoneware tiles form the back wall. All furniture - fronts are spatulated by hand to create a seemingly soft surface.

The polygonal kitchen block, also made of hand-brushed oak forms the room-filling conclusion and offers the residents a popular breakfast place. At the same time, it creates a calm, closed background for the dining area with its solid tabletop.

PH 56
SINDELFINGEN, GERMANY

Architecture: Architekten Lee+Mir
Client: confidential
Year of completion: 2019
No. of bedrooms: 2 rooms
Gross floor area: 300 m²
Wood: hand-brushed oak used for kitchen, sideboard dining area, wardrobe cabinet, dressing room, office sideboard and desk, bathroom furniture, doors

Furniture and floors made of brushed oak are complimented with black tiles.

The theme of black walls and details used in contrast to light, warm wood tones, translates to the upper floor. To this theme a greened moss-wall was added in the bathroom as an eye-catcher. On the upper floor, carpet flooring was used instead of wooden flooring to underline the cozy character of the office and bedroom.

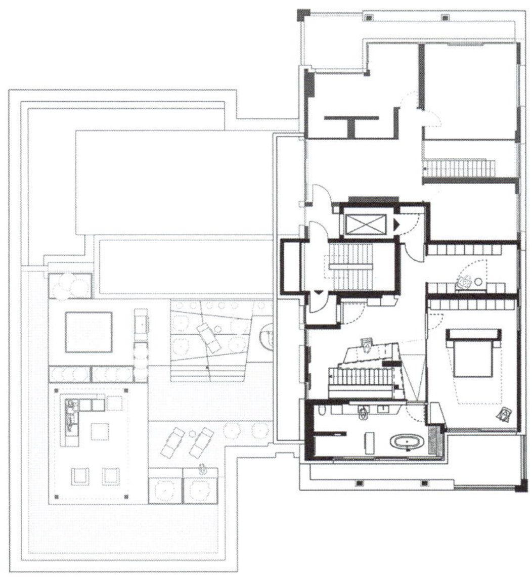

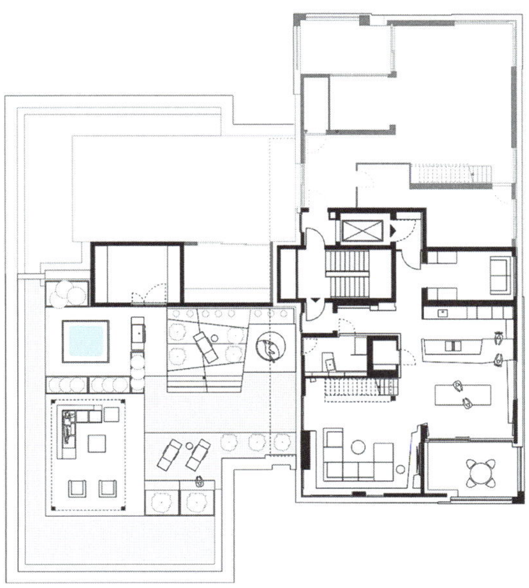

STRAW FLEA
MURSTETTEN, AUSTRIA

The property – the Schlcsspark in Murstetten – is an extraordinary place with historical significance and an eventful history. The special location is characterized by the direct proximity to the compact village center in the east and the fields and meadows in the west. The new building stands as a solitaire self-confidently and naturally in the midst of the historical remains.

The project is a single-room house, ranging in height from one to two stories. In the southern lower part is the living room with a large, hinged glazing to the garden and the small stream crossing the property. The building is entered through the northern part, where there is also a small sanitary unit and a sleeping gallery. The terrace in the south as well as the entrance stairs can be folded up by means of a cable pull, and the façades can thus be completely closed.

The large panoramic windows offer an unrestricted view of the remains of historical statues in the park. Along the long sides, the exterior walls are extended to the interior by a floor-to-ceiling shelf structure.

Architecture: juri troy architects
Participating offices: caravan atelier
Client: confidential
Year of completion: 2022
No. of bedrooms: 1 room
Gross floor area: 67 m²
Wood: untreated spruce used for façade, wooden beam construction, wall cladding, roof and floor, oiled spruce used for flooring, native coniferous wood used for wooden doors and window frames

The project follows a holistic sustainable concept in planning, use of materials and implementation.

The project follows a holistic sustainable concept. The house is elevated and only touches the terrain via the eight screw foundations, no ground area was sealed. The materials were mostly sourced in the immediate surroundings. The wood, both for the structural elements and for the surfaces, comes from the builder's own forests and was processed in the neighboring sawmill. The building is insulated with straw, which also comes from the immediate surroundings, from a regional farm. Heat and energy are generated by the photo-voltaic system on the roof.

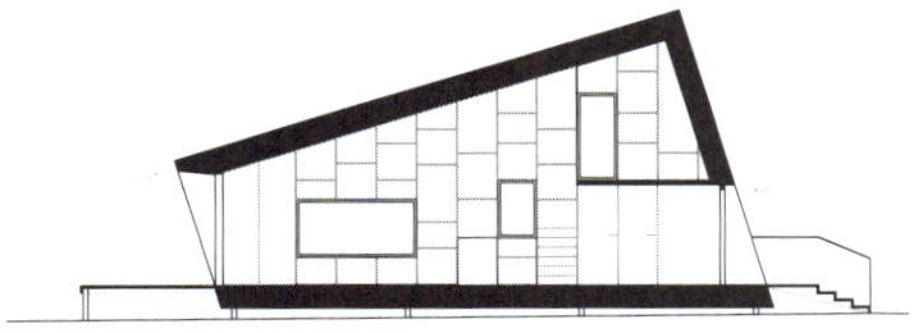

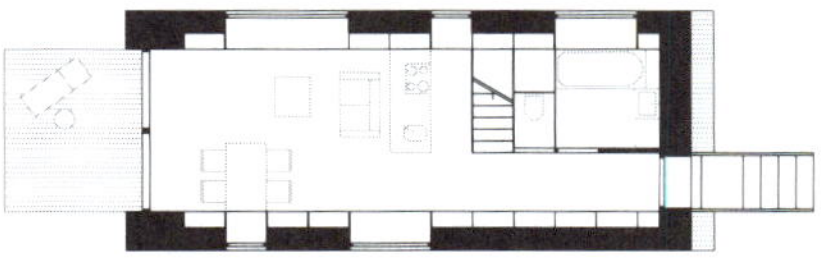

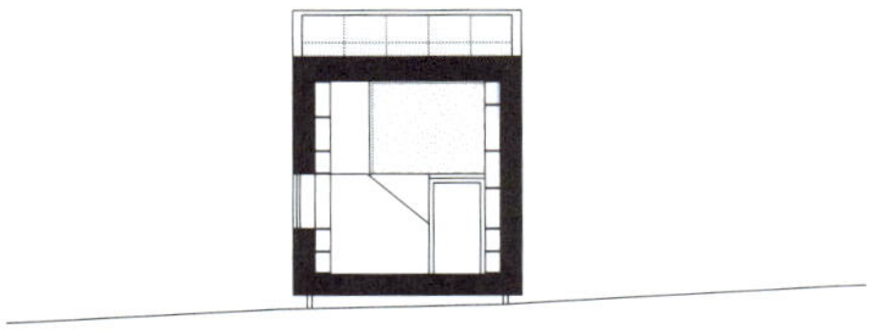

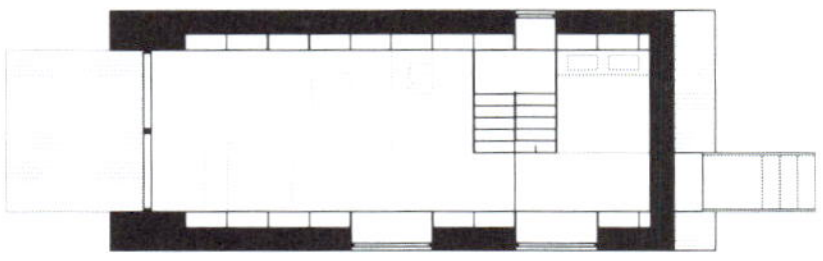

Two elongated volumes with pitched roofs are joined together at an angle and placed on the edge of the buildable area, defined by the setbacks. At first glance, this shape can appear to be reminiscent of the Beskydy region's typical small single-story home with a pitched roof. A south-facing private courtyard is formed inside the angle, protected from the north and overlooking a nearby forest. Shaded by the roof overhang, a wide deck stretching all the way along the house connects it with the courtyard, offering endless possibilities to sit, relax and listen to the sounds of running water, rustling leaves, or the distant hum of village life. Mature trees growing around the stream provide shade from the hot summer sun. The two wings intersect at the vestibule. This room gives a good overview of both wings, the courtyard and the deck, acting as a metaphoric entrance signpost. From the vestibule, on one side a door leads to the main living area, while on the other one enters a corridor to the in-law suite. The corridor goes along the east side of the annex and provides access to the mechanical room, the smaller bathroom and the grandparent's bedroom. It also connects this wing to the deck.

HOUSE WITH IN-LAW SUITE

RYBÍ, CZECH REPUBLIC

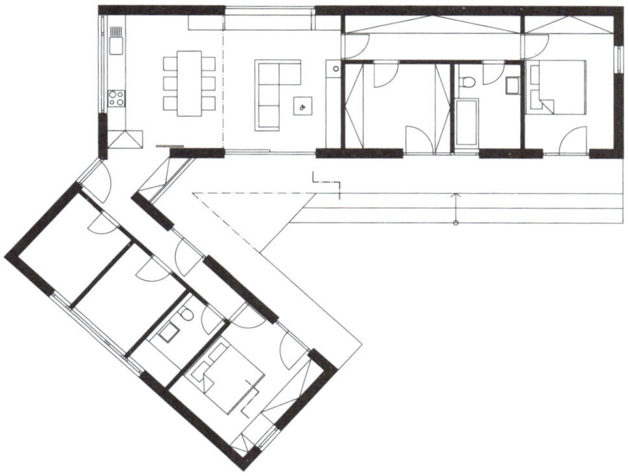

Architecture: KLAR / Václav Kocián, Zdeněk Liška
Client: confidential
Year of completion: 2021
No. of bedrooms: 4 rooms
Gross floor area: 145 m^2
Wood: spruce used for interior and structure, burnt spruce panels used for façade

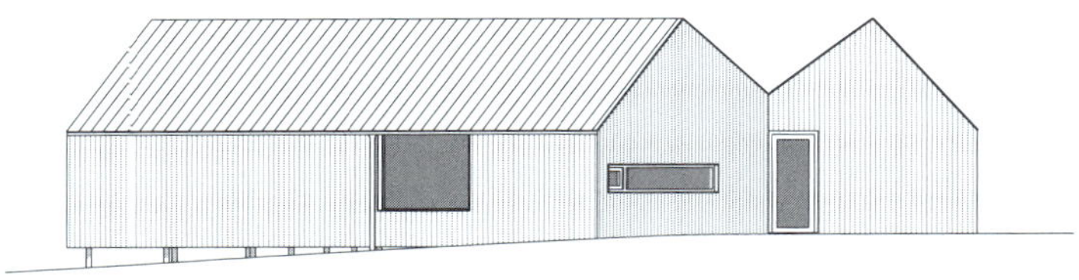

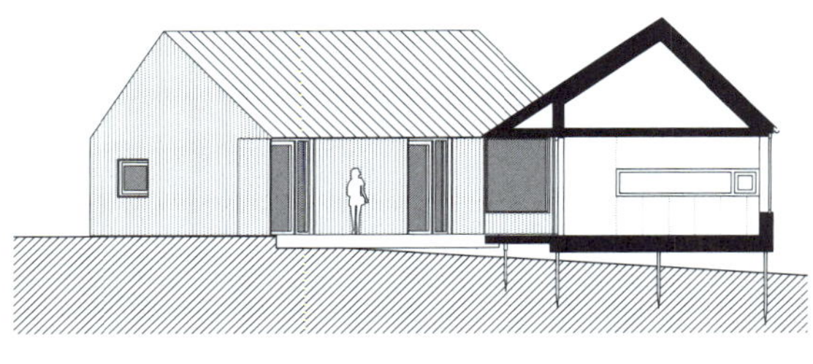

A corridor connects the living area with the private zone.

Entering the family wing from the vestibule, one reaches a double-height, open-plan living area with dining and cooking. Providing enough views inside and outside the house was emphasized here and everywhere around the building. From the cooking area, a horizontal strip window overlooks the entryway, while a wide window seat in the living area offers views of the landscape beyond. A corridor connects the living area with the private zone consisting of the children's bedroom, the main bathroom and the main bedroom. The open-plan living area and the bedrooms all have direct access to the deck.

The house is a home for a family partially build by the owners.

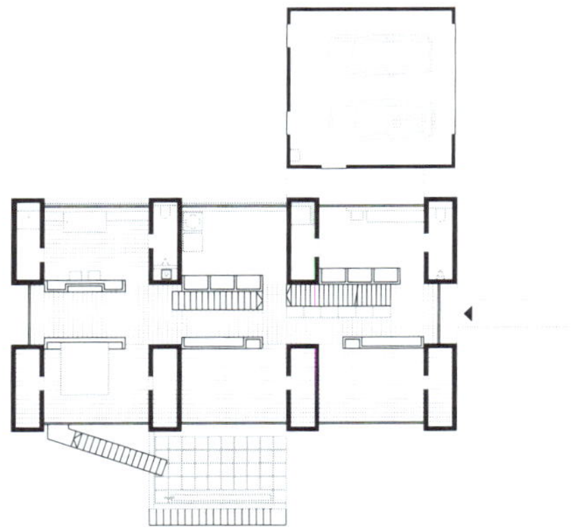

Architecture: Kühnlein Architektur
Client: confidential
Year of completion: 2021
No. of bedrooms: 3 rooms
Gross floor area: 487 m^2
Wood: 160 m^3 of spruce used for walls and ceilings, 160 m^2 of silver fir used for flooring, 277 m^2 of larch used for roof coverage

WOOD ON A SLOPE
SEUBERSDORF, GERMANY

This residential building with a garage is gently fitted into the tree population so that together with form and materiality it naturally rounds the entrance to the village. Closed blocks form a spatial frame with floor slabs. The floor plan structure is, like the historical Jura houses in the region, classically divided into three naves and three zones.

To take full advantage of the quality of the site on the western slope, the living rooms are located on the upper floor with a terrace. The bedrooms are placed on the first floor. A basement is necessary only in the downslope part of the house to accommodate the slope of the hillside. Here, the wooden pillars find a continuation with masonry natural stone plinths made of demolition material. An attached, flat gable roof summarizes the construction and conveys the familiar image of a classic house. The shell structure is identical on the ground floor and upper floor, with only the room-defining furniture creating differentiated spatial situations.

Gaps formed as main spaces seek a relationship with the landscape.

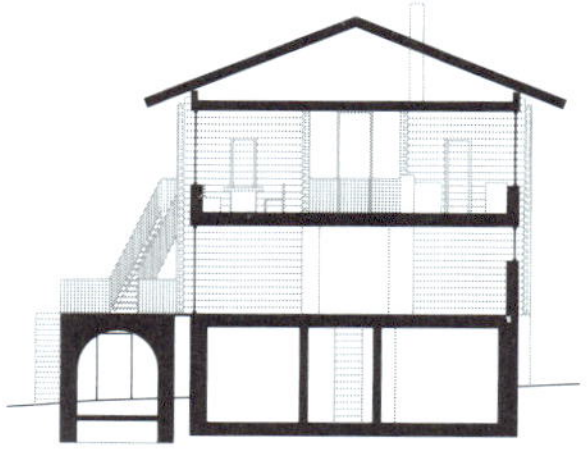

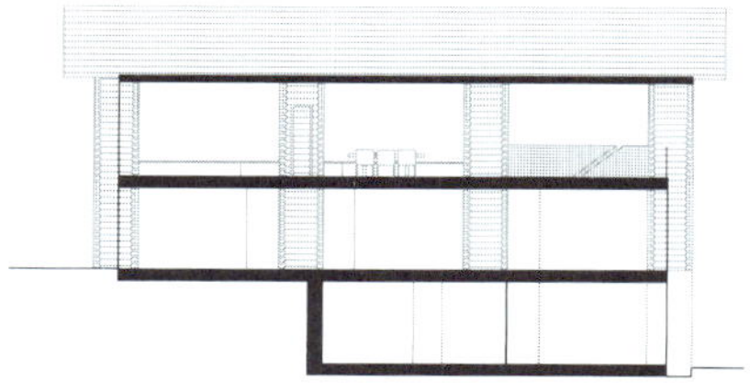

A soaped wooden floor made of silver fir completes the interior. All the construction timber was cut in the region, cut up in the local sawmill and tied and erected by the carpenter. The lighting is deliberately kept simple with black porcelain sockets, as are the black annealed surface-mounted light switches, outlets and hardware on windows and doors. A bold red accent is provided by the kitchen counter on the upper floor, which is the centerpiece of the home and features a kitchen and wood stove. An exterior vegetable earth cellar, also made of demolition stone, mediates between the upper and lower terraces.

ALEX
SINGAPORE, SINGAPORE

Alex, the name of the project as well as that of its owner, is a bachelor seeking a minimalist lifestyle with a wood-filled interior and a desk for Lego building. This new 47 square meter two-room public housing flat came with the standard compartmentalized areas for living, kitchen, bedroom, and bathroom. In a space for one, there is technically no need for doors within the flat.

Alex still has functional zones to play, work, sleep, cook and bathe, but without physical or visual demarcation between them such as changes in flooring material or height. Removing all internal walls and starting from a clean slate, the designer located them where they are most logical for the homeowner, and the resultant space is truly bespoke. To create openness and pared-down interiors the functional spaces were reconfigured, expressing them as a series of cuboid structures with a unified design language: This was realized as cabinetry. They were pushed against the flat's perimeter to optimize the common space.

Architecture: Spacedge Designs
Client: Alex Fong
Year of completion: 2020
No. of bedrooms: 1 room
Gross floor area: 47 m²
Wood: 58 m² of white elm laminate used for cuboid structures

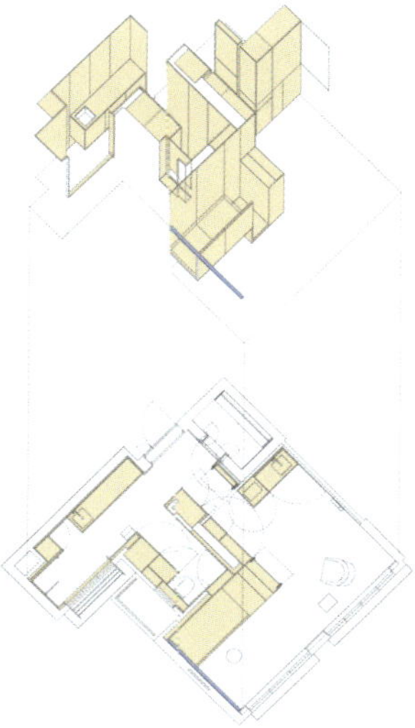

Open space was created with furniture that acts as a room divider.

The designer added a wall-hung coin bank spray-painted neon orange to meet feng shui requirements. The lighting too, a round blue metal tube with a diameter of 32 millimeters, traverses the space, creating clear and minimalistic lines throughout the interior.

The façade of black glazed larch covers the entire shape of the house. The façade is ventilated and screwed concealed. The black wood surface was also consistently used as the roof surface. The photo-voltaic panels are flush with the wooden surface of the roof. A change of material, which is not necessary, is not carried out. The garden is visually maximally connected to the living area by generous panoramic sliding doors with floor-to-ceiling glass panels. Transitions are fluid. The single-story house is threshold-free, so it accommodates all conditions, changes and generations.

The bathroom opens confidently to the outside through a floor-to-ceiling and room-wide glass panel. While showering, one can enjoy the view of the sky through a frameless skylight. Whether starlight or rainy mood, nature lets its changing light colors flow into the room. The ground floor slab has a concrete core-activated foundation slab that was smoothed to its finished state as it set, and the exposed concrete is only sealed.

HOUSE ANA
WÖRTH AM MAIN, GERMANY

Architecture: grams.grams architektur
Client: grams.grams architektur
Year of completion: 2020
No. of bedrooms: 3 rooms
Gross floor area: 160 m²
Wood: 240 m² of black varnished larch used for façade, 155 m² of black varnished larch used for roof cladding, 56 m² of natural douglas used for terrace

The house is heated by a geothermal heat pump and cooled in summer. A central ventilation system with heat recovery was installed, while a photo-voltaic system supplies the building with electricity. The building automation system adjusts all technical components according to weather conditions and demand so that no energy is senselessly wasted. The installed sensors record the outside and inside temperature, the humidity outside and inside, the brightness, the position of the sun, the wind speed and the temperature.

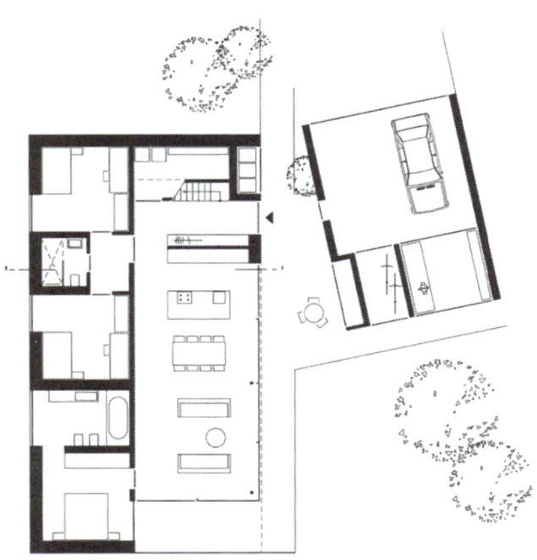

Black glazed larch covers the entire shape of the house.

THE SUN PATH HOUSE
KERNAVE, LITHUANIA

This house is situated in a small historic town called Kernave on the right bank of the river Neris, facing the old pine tree forest. The historic land with forests and hills creates a perfect area for an oasis to relax from the city hustle. This house was created as a getaway for a young family of four to spend their weekends and holidays in. Since the site is in a highly protected area, the new project had to meet strict regulations regarding construction, building area, height and even the roof angle had to meet certain requirements.

The most important architectural task was to maintain modern architectural expression. While creating the house a lot of attention has been paid to outdoor spaces and their connection with nature. Large, forest-facing windows erase the barrier between the interior and the exterior, creating a maximum connection with the natural atmosphere. Three designed terraces follow the path of the sun: morning coffee and awakening nature can be enjoyed on the east terrace, the covered south terrace is perfect for midday sun, and the west forest-facing terrace is where the hustle and bustle of the day calm down and the sunset can be enjoyed.

Architecture: Lunaarch
Client: confidential
Year of completion: 2022
No. of bedrooms: 4 rooms
Gross floor area: 145 m^2
Wood: 265 m^2 of thermal wood used for façade and terraces, 280 m^2 of pine used for interior walls and ceilings, 150 m^2 of oak used for floors

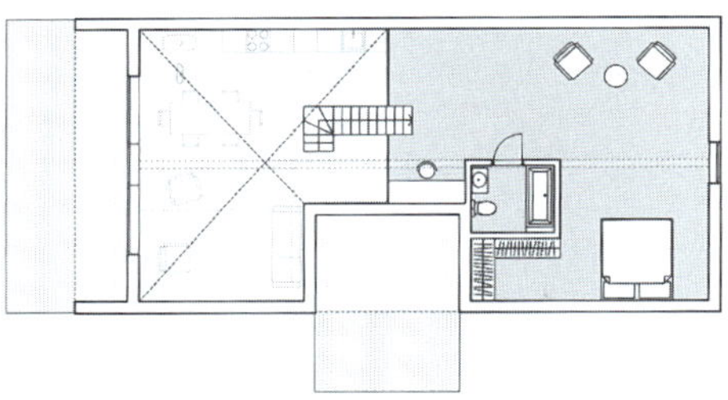

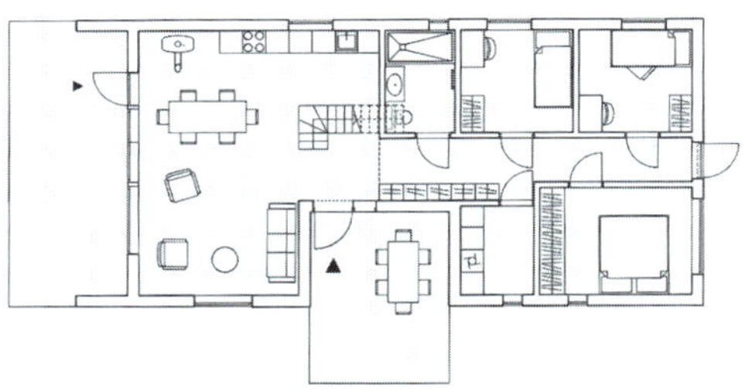

Located on a historical site, this shed provides comfort during stressful days.

Regarding the site plan, the house is built on top of the hill, which opens up to the best view of the forest. All site area is divided into different zones. The forest side is for leisure time, it is where the main terraces open up and the natural pool is located. The eastern side is for gardening with a greenhouse and special planting boxes for a small vegetable garden. There is nothing unnecessary either inside or outside the house: only practical and functional furniture and appliances. It gives a sense of space and does not interfere with enjoying the beauty of nature.

MAISON D'ARTISTE
THIELLE, SWITZERLAND

This house is located in the garden of an old farm. The layout is flexible and contains an artist's studio that can easily be converted into housing on a minimal surface distributed over two communicating levels and without excavation. The proposed minimalist architecture is spatial, contextual and contemporary. At the same time, it was built to be functional, economical and ecological. Maison d'Artiste is made of prefabricated structural elements in wood for quick assembly. The details and finishing touches are left to the owners and have been designed so that they can be worked on by them. The ventilated façades are placed in a playful and random way to create frames on the site. The entrance is marked by a raw metal eave that recalls the material from the rural environment and reworked by the sculptor Ivan Freymond.

Architecture: maison d'art'chitecture serge grard
Client: Sylvie Nicoud and Ivan Freymond
Year of completion: 2022
No. of bedrooms: 4 rooms
Gross floor area: 78 m²
Wood: 128 m² of pre-aged spruce used for façades, 310 m² of natural spruce used for laminated beams, walls, shelves and ceilings in 3-ply panels

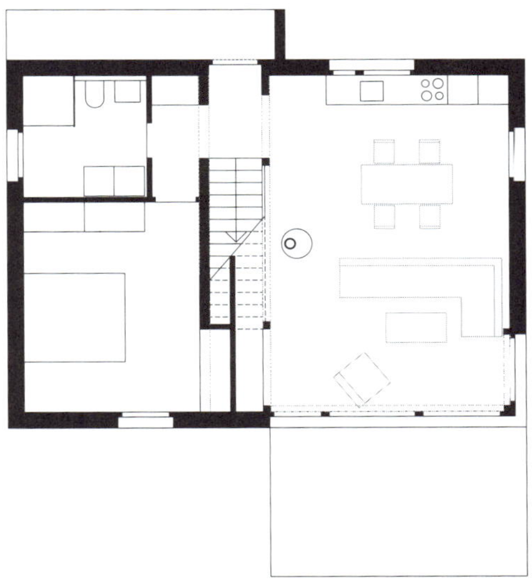

This house offers variability: It serves as an artist's office and can be transformed into a living space.

Room for storage was built under the stairs directly with the construction of the house. The overal design of the house plays with a mix of materials in color and form. Natural wood is matched and contrasted with black details and sculptural iron ornaments. The gray wooden façade is supplemented with the iron entrance frame.

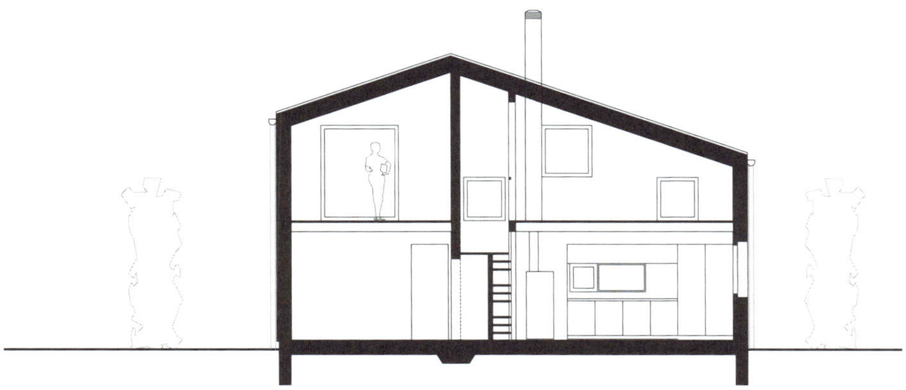

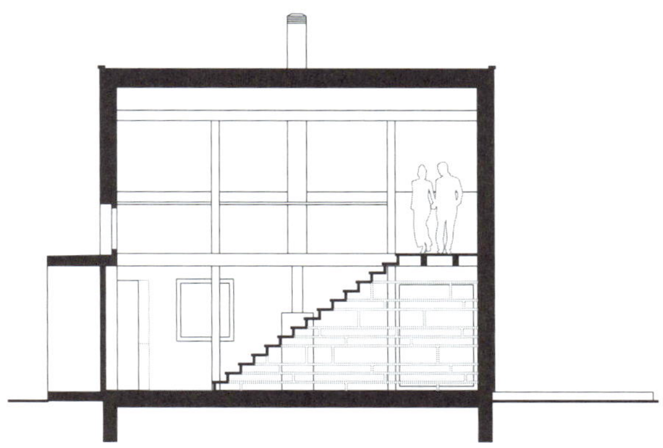

SU-PIDER
FUKUYAMA-CITY, JAPAN

This house for a family of four in a suburban residential area is located in a hilly region. The surrounding environment is a uniform landscape with houses built parallel to a plot and with a certain aspect ratio characteristic of residential areas. The north side of the property faces the street, while the east and west sides are on a slope with a slight difference in elevation from the neighboring properties. The property is also characterized by a graded topography created by a large difference in elevation to the south. Considering that the property is vacant under the south-west side of the plot, the entire volume is angled at forty-five degrees to the terrain to create an expansive environment with desirable views, ventilation, natural light and privacy.

Specifically, an octagonal spiderweb-shaped structure is roofed over extending down from the top to the supporting legs to create a centripetal single space. The legs support at four points, and the interior and exterior are connected by triangular openings that link the vertices between the pivots. Inside the large open space, four boxes that don't serve as rooms are arranged to create a corridor-like area that functions as a family room and living space.

Architecture: UID architects and Keisuke Maeda
Structural design: Takashi Manda Structural Design
Landscape design: Toshiya Ogino Landscape Design
Client: confidential
Year of completion: 2020
No. of bedrooms: 4 rooms
Gross floor area: 77.07 m²
Wood: engineered wood used for girders, douglas fir used for beams, lauan plywood and structural plywood used for floors, walls and ceilings

Privacy is created through corners and elevated spaces.

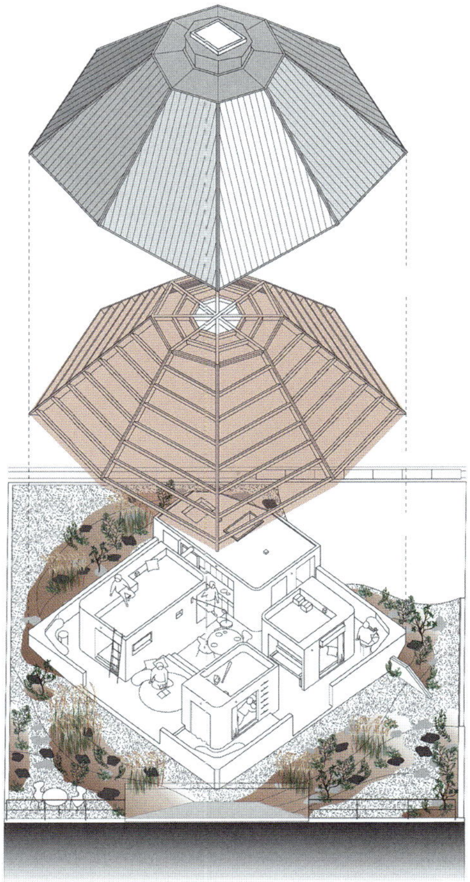

There are few closed rooms, but family members can pursue their hobbies in the open space.

The space can be neat and tidy or completely cluttered. Since there is no structure that defines a particular area as a room, the areas and patterns within the room are likely to change over time as children grow older and other changes occur in the family's life. It is a home with strong architectural features that accommodate the changes in the daily life of a family with a unique lifestyle.

This house was designed for an owner who wanted not only a comfortable but also practical living space in the center of a hectic city. As with their past projects, Mia Design Studio has done its best to create more space as the actual living space for people which is becoming smaller due to urbanization. The first thing was to reduce the requirement to the point that meets the client's needs, nothing more, nothing less. And from there, they created a large garden, rather than just a few small green zones at the entrance or front door.

The main concept was to create a living space that floats above a mini-garden and gives the feeling of walking on bridges. All the main activities in the house are connected by the empty zone between plants, water and daylight. Another special feature is the location next to the historical buildings of Sai Gon. It is also located in the middle of a dense district of the city. In the early dawn or dusk, one can clearly hear the church bell and walking a few steps out of the house, one will directly come into contact with the ambiance of Sai Gon alley, which can be seen as a unique feature of the city's culture.

VILLA TAN ĐINH
HO CHI MINH CITY, VIETNAM

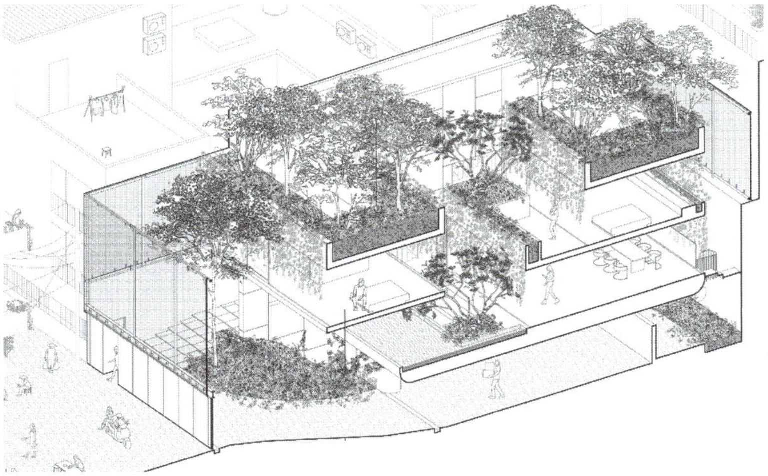

Architecture: MIA Design Studio
Client: confidential
Year of completion: 2020
No. of bedrooms: 3 rooms
Gross floor area: 538.29 m^2
Wood: 154,7 m^2 of oak used for floor finishing
75,6 m^2 of ash used for staircase and wooden book shelves

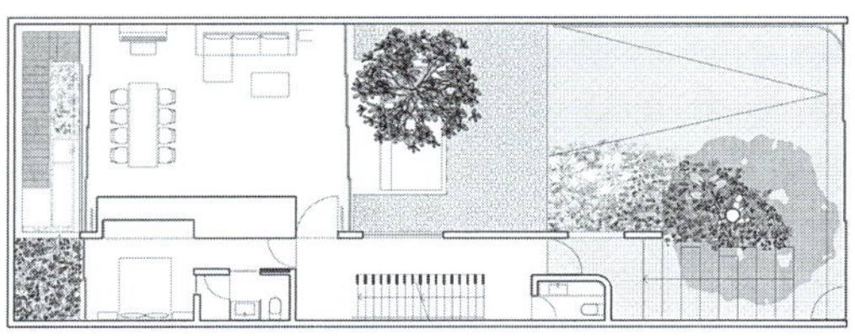

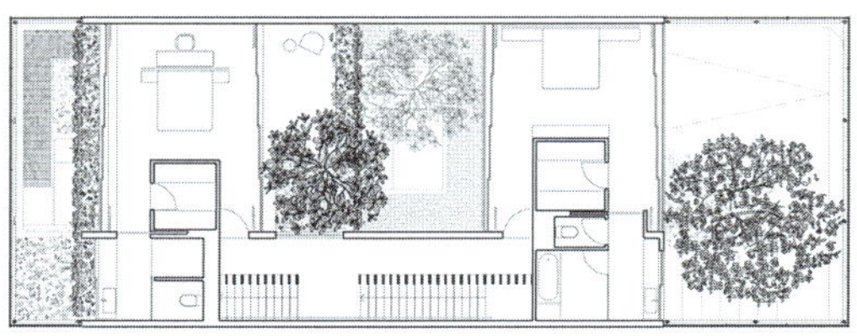

The house almost functions as a small eco-system filled with plants.

With this in mind, the design team has created a thin steel cover that delineates the private spaces and captures the most distinctive areas. Plants spread over the steel mesh system, creating a fresh green filter for the house. From the outside, the house could be considered a simple box but from the inside it contains many layers of spaces as well as an alternation between light and dark, intertwined with the raw material of concrete, stones and especially wood.

DECKHOUSE
NORTHERN VERMONT, VT, USA

Deckhouse is a custom home on Lake Champlain inspired by its vibrant maritime history. Conceptually, the house reflects the nautical lines and materiality of a wooden vessel. The program outlined a five-bedroom home with an existing boathouse on the property to be renovated. The unique site features of the lake, mountain views and exposed ledge, coupled with desired privacy from an adjacent public park, informed the siting and organization of the home.

The application of wood cladding and detailing was paramount for the execution of the concept. Certified ipe was chosen as singular material for the project. After many iterations of different wood species, ipe was chosen for its longevity, natural weathering patina, durability and consistency of grain.

The project walls, roof, decking, and soffits are clad entirely of the ipe. Thoughtful consideration of maintaining the purity of the wooden form informed the unique details of the exterior. In response to this, many functional aspects of building components were concealed within the architecture. The wall detailing is part rain screen, part conventional siding. The rain screen layer provides a scrim wall concealing the downspouts from the roof collection. The wood roof is a rain screen, concealing the water collection system within the roof eaves.

Architecture: Birdseye
Interior design: Jack Fhillips Design
Landscape design: Wagner Hodgson Landscape Architecture
Client: confidential
Year of completion: 2020
No. of bedrooms: 5 rooms
Gross floor area: 744 m^2
Wood: 2,875 m^2 of ipe used for exterior wall and roof cladding
400 m^2 of ipe used for exterior decking

The ipe was sourced through a local lumber company that provided third-party analysis by Living Forest of the chain of custody. The material was certified, meeting the criteria for licensing, harvesting, transporting, product volume, labor practices, and company ethics.

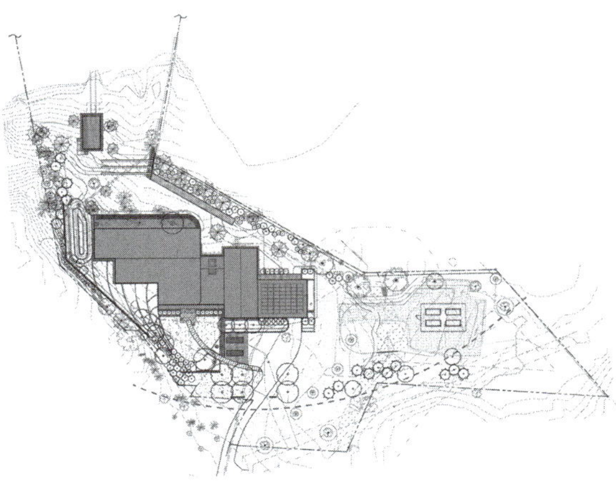

White oak was used for the interior wall paneling and floor covering.

The aim of the project Home Urban Home is to house an artist associated with the Conde Duque, providing him with both a workplace and a temporary home. The final location is a bright corner of only 18 square meters in the lobby of the theater on the second floor. Before moving the Home Urban Home to its final location, it had to be built in the center of the main courtyard so that it could be visited by the public during the Madrid Design Festival. The actual house consists of a minimal wooden box where one can sleep, eat, work or relax. This is part of the larger construction.

A small cell, serving as an intermediate space, was inserted in a semi-transperent house. A space full of light and nature, where the floor can be hard, sloping or even unstable, where people can climb, change levels and wander. The house-within-the-house-idea allows the creation of two almost opposite environments by combining two very different materials such as polycarbonate and wood. The inner house is a shelter, opaque, warm and insulated. The outer skin is luminous, bright and transparent, a place with vegetation, where one can look at the sunset in the city.

HOME URBAN HOME
MADRID, SPAIN

Architecture: MYCC
Client: Mini Spain – BMW Group
Year of completion: 2019
No. of bedrooms: 1 room
Gross floor area: 35.57 m²
Wood: 115.56 m³ of fir used for structure, 33.4 m² of poplar plywood used for living room, kitchen, garden, bedroom and attic

MINI

The tree emphasizes the beauty of nature in union with architecture.

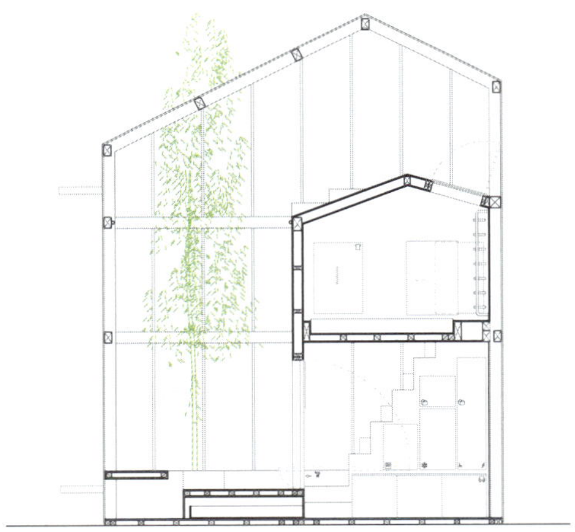

Children are free to roam and play in the dollhouse.

It is a succession and overlapping of spaces with their own material qualities, versatile enough to accommodate a variety of creative activities where the user gets to decide and the architecture does not impose itself. The silhouette of the volume is not random. It deliberately evokes the house that a child would draw to evoke home, giving the user the feeling of being at home for a few days, despite being in the lobby of a theater. Moreover, this simple and iconic form brings back childhood memories.

BOSVILLA
BERGEN, THE NETHERLANDS

Hidden in the wooden coastal area of the old artist town of Bergen Natrufied Architecture designed a house, a garden house, a carport and a bike storage in an undulating dune landscape. The intentions for the design were to embed and create living spaces in balance with nature. After mapping heights and trees, the buildings were carefully laid out to enclose nature to its fullest.

The main house has a completely open floor plan set between oak and pine trees and the big roof lets in sun in evening and winter settings, while protecting the inhabitants from the hotter hours. The cantilevering roof also provides for covered outdoor seating within the natural setting, including an outdoor fireplace. The floor plan has open and more secluded areas to provide for different needs during the day. Big revolving and sliding doors provide uninterrupted access to the outside terraces, making outside and inside spaces flow into each other easily. Hidden in the sandy soil, the bedroom area has windows towards the forest, providing maximum privacy, while a grid at the south side lets twinkling sunlight enter the bathroom.

Architecture: Natrufied Architecture
Interior design: DIS studio
Client: Tom Stolk and Maaike Groot
Year of completion: 2018
No. of bedrooms: 4 rooms
Gross floor area: 400 m^2
Wood: laminated iroko used for main structure, jatoba used for wooden window frames, afrormosia used for ceiling panels, bamboo used for bedroom flooring, doors and door frames

Nature seeps from the outside right into the building.

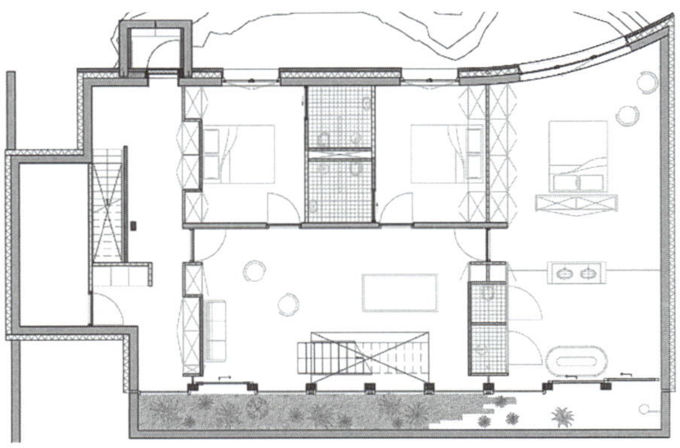

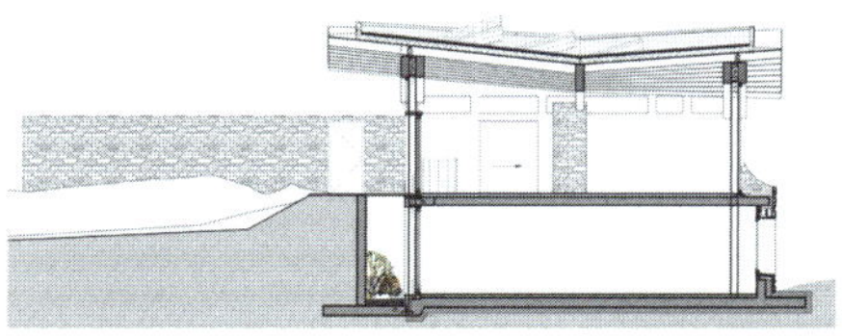

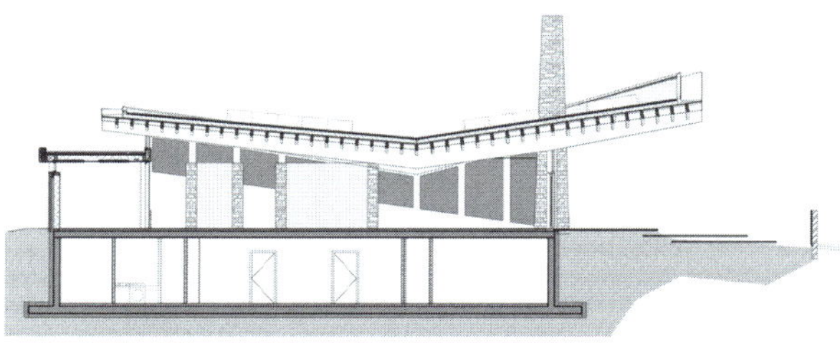

Different types of carbon absorbing materials were chosen to make the house carbon friendly.

Columns and beams are made of laminated FSC-iroko, the substructure of local pine wood, window and doorframes of FSC-jatoba, the ceiling of FSC-afrormosia, interior (sliding) doors and doorframes of bamboo, stairs, ground floor and terraces are made out of FSC-afzelia, and the wood façade of FSC-cumaru. This collection of wood gives a soft palette of natural tones, together with materials like brass, copper and Belgian flagstones. A green wall in the basement gives an extra twist to living in nature.

KLEINE BLEIBE
MONTABAUR, GERMANY

The Kleine Bleibe, German for "small stay", is an ensemble of two vacation houses and a sauna house. Half-timbered houses standing under monument protection characterize the image of the village, where the Kleine Bleibe is located. The architecture of the houses blends traditional construction with timeless architecture. The solid base and the black wooden façade of the cottages are a tribute to the traditional building style found in the surrounding area. In line with the traditional building culture, the houses have a roof overhang. Thus, the small abode fits perfectly into the local landscape, and yet bears its own signature.

Vacations in a simple and sustainable form is the core idea to which the timeless architecture of the vacation homes should give expression. Discreet details, high-quality materials and a purist style are intended to radiate peace and balance.
The height and layout of the vacation homes have been chosen so that when one looks out of the window one can see the surrounding landscape and nature.

Architecture: Fröhlich Gassner Architekten
Client: confidential
Year of completion: 2022
No. of bedrooms: 3 rooms
Gross floor area: 170 m^2
Wood: 130 m^3 of middle European spruce used for walls, ceilings, roof, façade, insulation, windows, furniture, 2 m^3 of silver fir used for floor

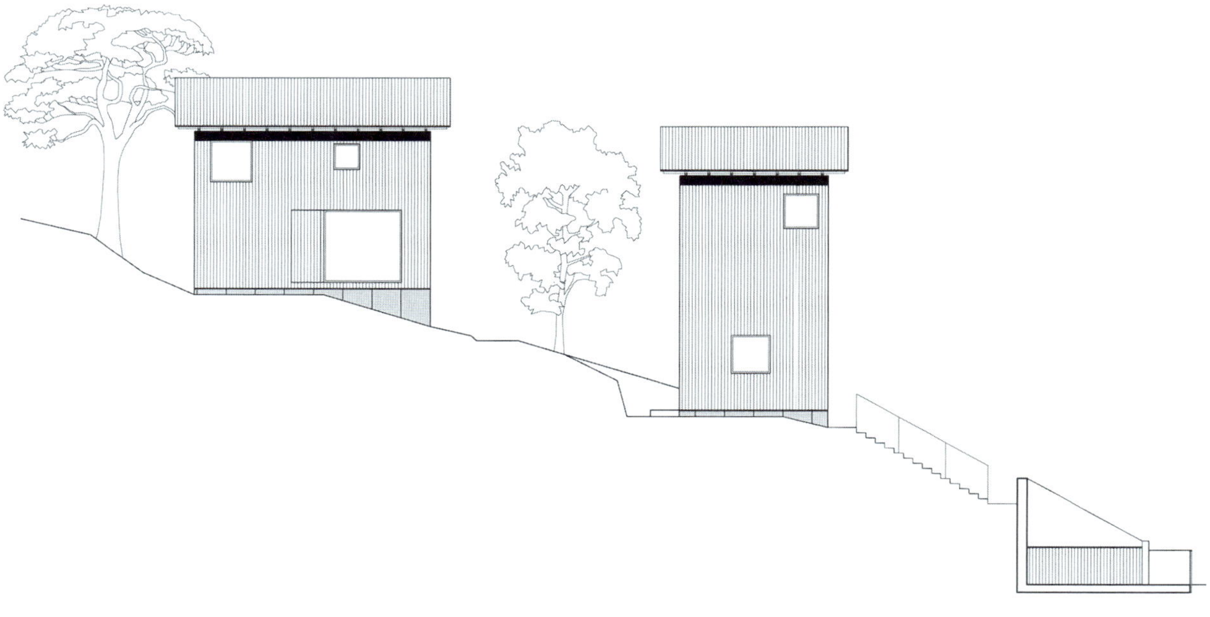

Utility trees line the surroundings of the cottages. The houses were placed in such a way that the existing plum and walnut trees were not endangered. The cottages are built to be sturdy yet resource friendly. Walls, ceilings and roofs are made of cross-laminated timber. The interiors feature solid wood planks, robustly sanded screed and water-resistant tiles. All pathways, terraces and parking areas feature a percolating surface.

A blend of tradition and timeless architecture in balance with landscape and natural surroundings.

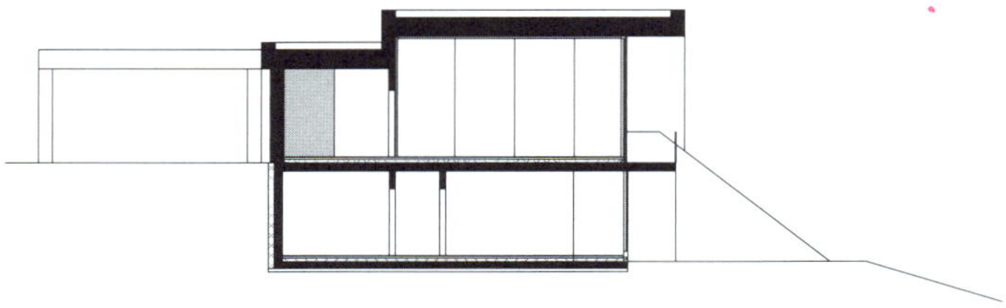

Architecture: Schiller Architektur
Client: confidential
Year of completion: 2022
No. of bedrooms: 3 rooms
Gross floor area: 300 m²
Wood: KVH spruce used for construction, outside walls, roof Spruce used for windows, brushed and oiled oak used for flooring , white fir used for façade

FAMILY HOME CL16
FILSTAL, GERMANY

The building is located on a southern slope of the Filstal valley. Below an old tree population protects the house from view and gives a frame to the view over the valley.

To form a kind of courtyard, the garage and residential building are set at a 90-degree angle to each other, separated by a joint that allows a passage to the terrace. To enhance the entrance, it was set back and ensures protected access into the building. The residential building was structured in a grid pattern, which is also reflected in the external shape of the structure. Thanks to complete openness and generous room height, the living, dining and kitchen area is reminiscent of a hall and offers a far-reaching view to the south through extensive glazing. The north side, on the other hand, is closed on one side in order to exclude glimpses of the higher neighboring buildings. The stairwell on the north side is lit by a skylight.

Two downward-pointing braces of silver fir enclose the structure; the area within the braces is filled with glass and dark fiber cement. Floor slabs and walls of the basement are made of raw exposed concrete. White walls, ceilings of exposed concrete, and floors of parquet and tiles are complemented by Le Corbusier colors. The colorful and artistic decoration and furniture of the builders further enliven the building.

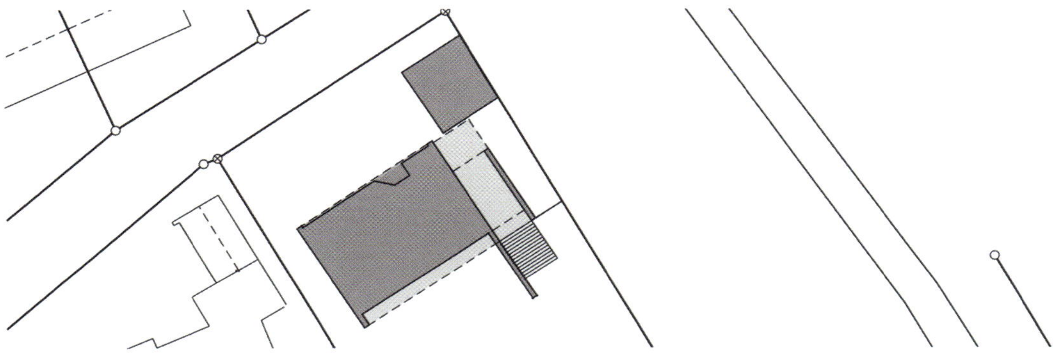

Overall, emphasis was placed on naturalness of materials.

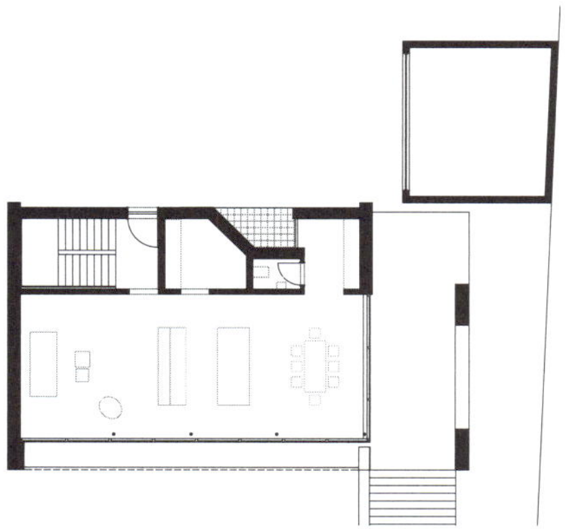

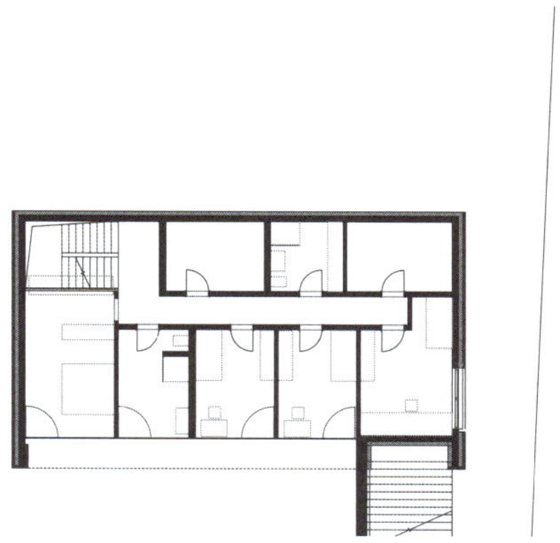

Architecture: Katja Knaus Freie Architektin
Client: confidential
Year of completion: 2020
No. of bedrooms: 3 rooms
Gross floor area: 200 m^2
Wood: 93 m^3 of untreated fir, spruce and cross laminated timber used for walls, ceilings and roof in visible quality, 12 m^3 of black and untreated silver fir used for façade, 89 m^3 of wood fiber insulation, 30 m^3 of various wood types used for windows and other elements

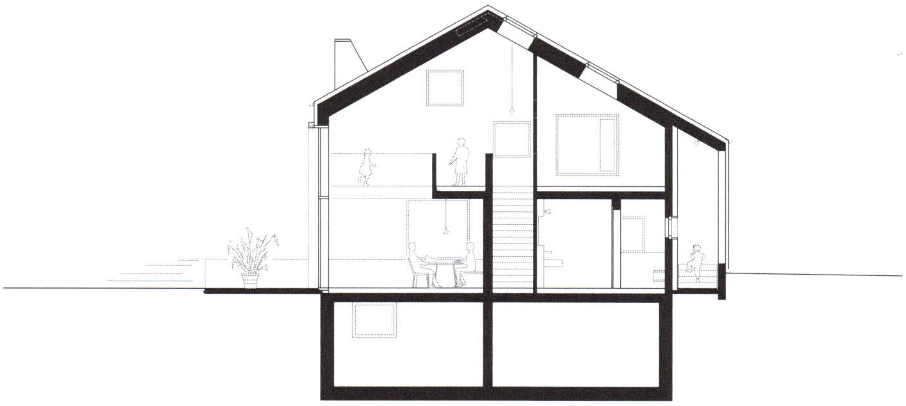

HOFHAUS
HOTZENWALD, GERMANY

The dwelling house is located in the Hotzenwald, on the family land formerly used for agriculture. The small hamlet, located on a hill, has now been supplemented by six residential houses. The outer wing of the economic part remains in the form of a shed. The remaining economic part is cut out and used as an inner courtyard. The inner courtyard enables a wind- and visibility-protected stay outside. The house has a closed, barn-like character to the north while to the south it reveals and opens itself as a residential house. There one has a free view of flower meadows and fruit trees to the mountain panorama of the Swiss Alps.

The shed is used as storage for wood and corresponding equipment. This is because the builder cuts the wood himself in the forest for the log heating system. As a modern shed, however, this additionally offers an outdoor seating area, the outdoor living room. A reinforced concrete core as a storage mass is encased in a solid wood structure. All surfaces are left raw. Windows and façade are made of silver fir. The façade is kept simple, the only design element si black cutouts. The diamond-shaped decorative cuts quote familiar elements of agricultural buildings in the Black Forest.

Furthermore, guest rooms, the seating niche "Stube" with tiled stove "Chunscht" and the kitchen with dining table surround the core. The large dining table is located in a so-called "Allraum" with air space and a panoramic window. The upper floor is accessed via the concrete staircase first to the gallery where people play and read. To the right is the workroom. Views through the air space, various glass cutouts in the room partitions and the open floor plan connect the two floors and let them become one whole.

Large openings allow the omnipresence of the outside landscape.

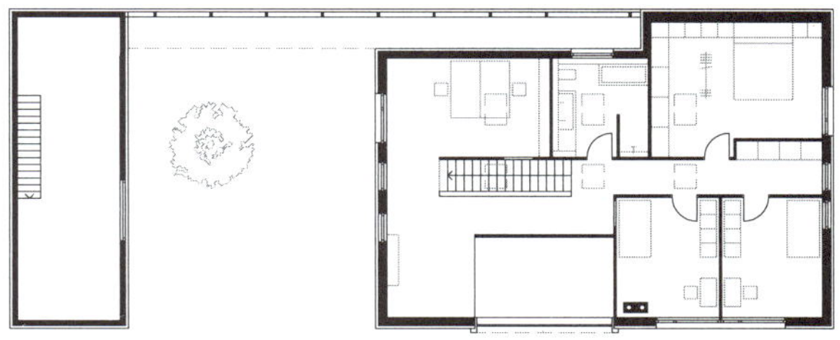

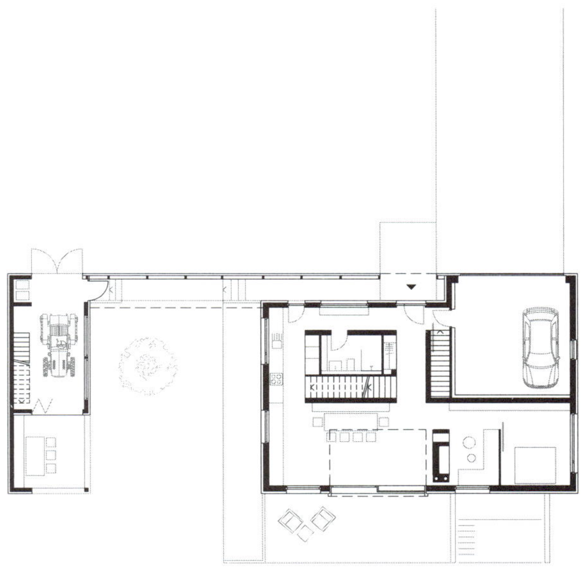

At an altitude of 1,000 meters in the Upper Black Forest, an existing wooden shed was converted into a small single-family house, which is part of a listed farm dating from 1659. The outer shell of this tiny house called La Chalette includes the roofing that was preserved. Only a few interventions, such as the bay windows in the façade, indicate from the outside that a conversion has taken place here. The existing openings, the large barn door and the wooden door on the valley side, now serve as shutters for the new generous fixed glazing with glass doors.

Inside, the building was completely insulated according to the german KfW 85 standard. It is fitted with native silver fir cladding. Silver fir triple-layer panels were used for the bathroom and kitchen walls and ceilings. The living area has a wooden floor made of silver fir, the bathroom and kitchen have each received a tile floor. On the valley side, one enters the kitchen with its cozy sitting area via the covered wooden terrace. Adjacent there is a bathroom, which provides a view from the bathtub into the landscape.

LA CHALETTE
LENZKIRCH, GERMANY

Architecture: Ohlf Schoch Architekten
Client: Martin Ohlf und Christine Müller-Welt
Year of completion: 2020
No. of bedrooms: 1 room
Gross floor area: 55 m^2
Wood: oiled silver fir, knotless rift used for floor, windows, doors, interior cladding, sloping roof and façade

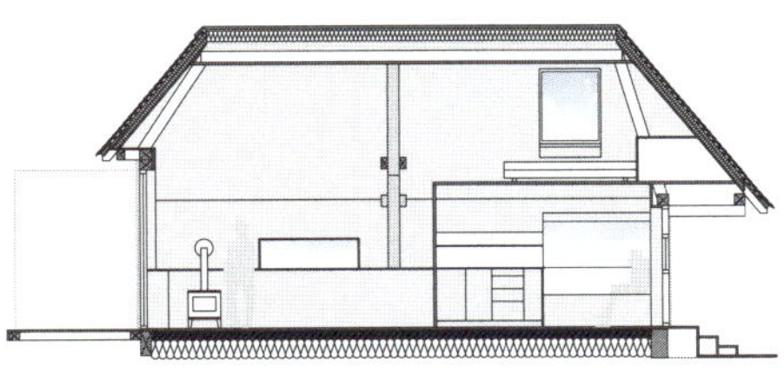

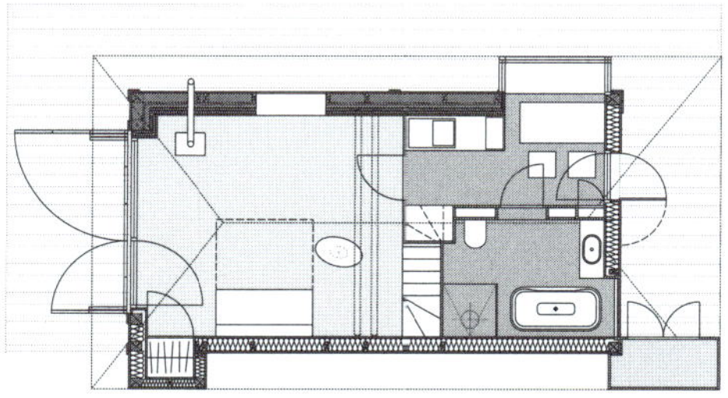

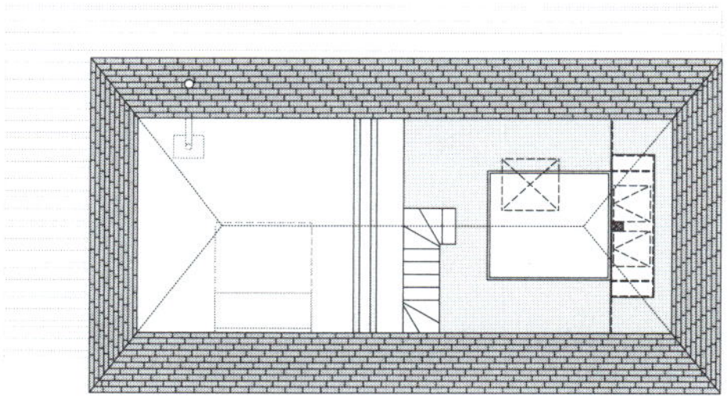

This tiny timber home forms a cozy shelter without loosing touch with nature.

The kitchen opens up to the two-story living area with its front terrace made of natural stone and a wide view of the landscape. From this living area, the sleeping level is accessed via a wooden staircase, which is located above the kitchen and bath area and is lit by a skylight. The house is heated via a solar fan and can also be fired with wood by a fireplace.

THE HANGING HOUSE
CAMPOS NOVOS PAULISTA, BRAZIL

The Hanging House was named this way because it is elevated from the natural ground level of the site where it is located. This is because the house is surrounded by native trees, so the windows are leveled with the treetops and the balconies blend in with the branches. In addition, the soil remains original, preserving the drainage and root dynamics, which were not harmed because a minimal amount of concrete was used in the foundations.

The project's premise was a country house that is integrated with the local ecosystem, with sustainability and recyclability. For this reason, the construction system with recycled maritime containers was adopted by Daniel Assuane Duarte and Nadia Barros Assuane. In total, 80 percent of the materials are recycled. Internally, demolition wood predominates in the walls and ceiling. Green roofs with rainwater reuse and thermal and acoustic insulation are also the highlights of the house.

The raised ground floor features the common areas of the house, living spaces, leisure and balconies. In total, there are two bedrooms and two bathrooms. The house has no television or wifi system. To inhabit it, the rule is to disconnect and enjoy what nature and family life provide. Two wooden deck balconies provide interaction with native trees and fantastic views of the rural area of Campos Novos Paulista, Brazil.

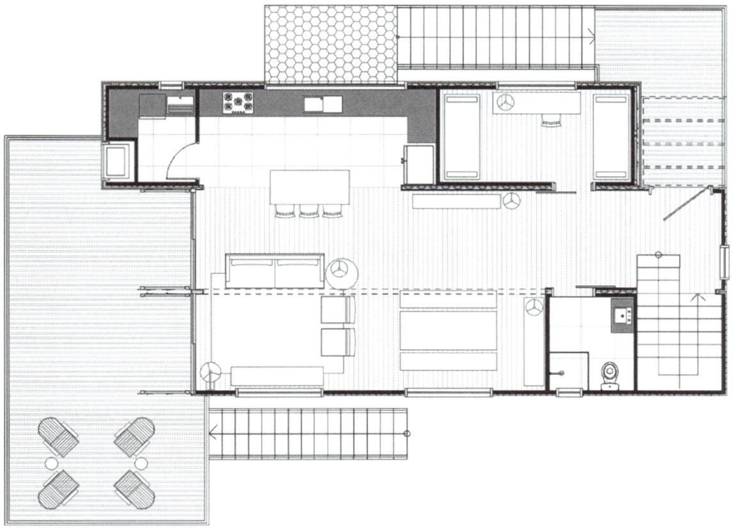

Architecture: Barros Assuane Arquitetura
Client: confidential
Year of completion: 2019
No. of bedrooms: 2 rooms
Gross floor area: 257 m²
Wood: reclaimed peroba rosa used for interior cladding, peroba mica for decks

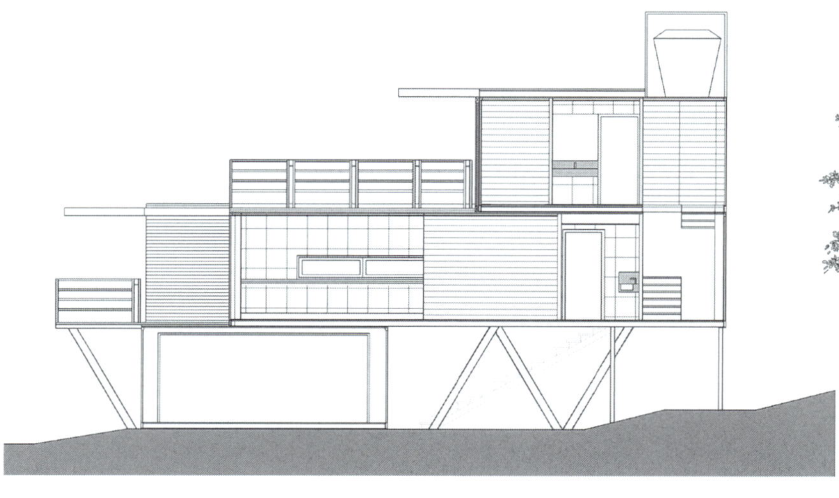

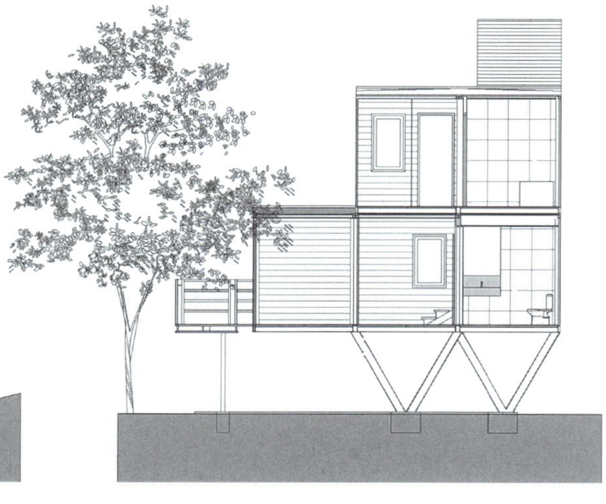

The internal divisions are in demolition wood. Besides being a recycled material, it avoids the use of internal painting, since it already has its own finish.

The foundations are shallow because the weight of the house is relatively light.

All walls of the house are insulated with thermo-acoustic blankets for thermal comfort. The environments have cross ventilation and wide openings for air exchange and thermal comfort. The house has no air conditioning system and remains pleasant even on the hottest days in Sao Paulo State. The internal doors of the first floor of the house are made with reused plates of the cutouts of the containers, minimizing excess material.

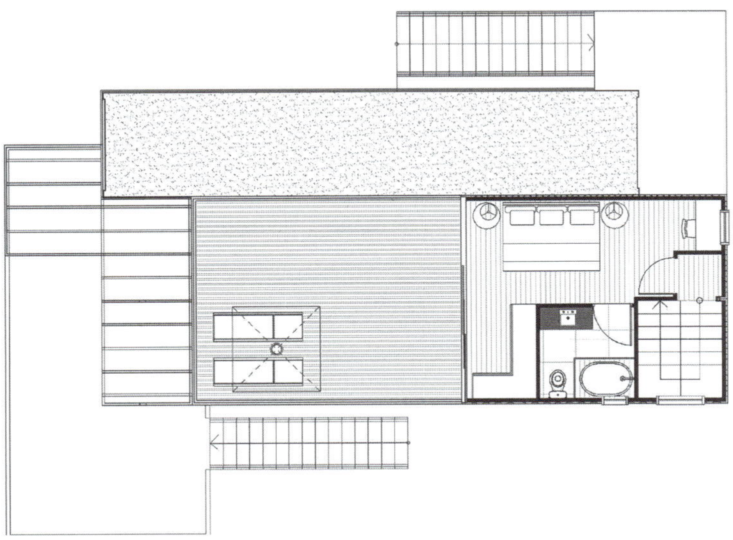

The Wooden Villa is a see-through heaven inviting the beauty of its surrounding environment inside. The floor and the ceiling mirror each other's dimensions, breaking down all notions of hierarchy. The eyesight glides between pine trees and interior perspectives, the feet move with ease from the warm sand – outside – to the soft okoumé wooden floor – inside. The pine and oak trees provide shelter frcm strong winds. Nature runs through the bedrooms and the living room. In order to redefine the threshold, there is no traditional front entrance.

The roof is made out of larch caissons, the matching floor with this time 136 okoume wood panels, all in perfect symmetry: an architectural sandwich. The sliding glass doors reach almost up to the roof, three meters high, opening the house to the outside surroundings. The shadows of the pine forest, projected onto the interior wooden surfaces, accompany the inhabitants with different degrees of intensity throughout the day. The bedrooms and living room make the most of all four cardinal directions, north, east, south and west.

THE WOODEN VILLA
SOULAC-SUR-MER, FRANCE

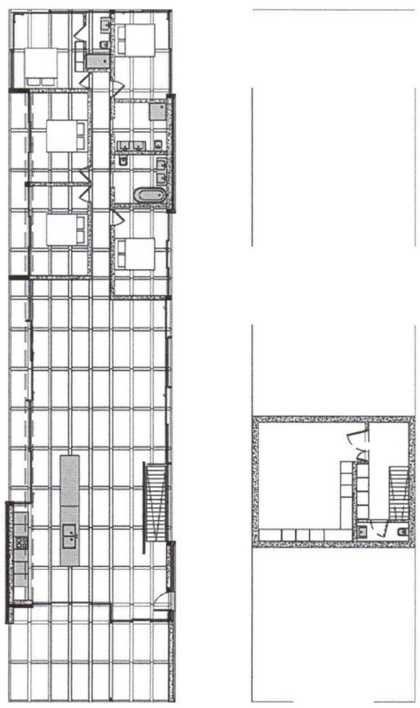

Architecture: Nicolas Dahan Architects
Client: confidential
Year of completion: 2020
No. of bedrooms: 5 rooms
Gross floor area: 250 m²
Wood: oak used for furniture and stairs, larch used for ceiling structures, okoume used for floors and walls

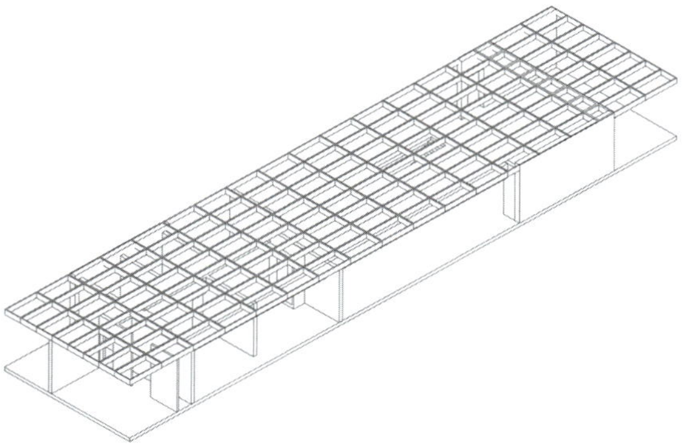

Two-thirds of the house are built using glass walls that are too light to hold down the roof in heavy weather. The house is weighed down with metal and anchored with cement walls. The wood and glass are pushed to their limits, in such a way that they reveal their strengths and weaknesses. The house is a member of the family in the Japanese sense, a member that must be taken care of.

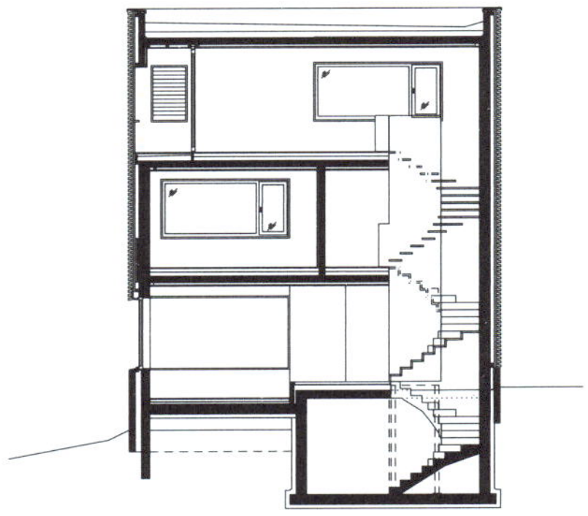

Architecture: firm Architekten
Client: confidential
Year of completion: 2020
No. of bedrooms: 3 rooms
Gross floor area: 240 m²
Wood: 450 m³ of spruce used for construction, walls, ceiling, façade, 20 m³ of silver fir used for furniture, acoustic ceiling, 130 m² of beech used for flooring, 4 m³ of elm used for furniture

HOUSE IN THE ORCHARD
FRASTANZ, AUSTRIA

In the district of Gampelün in Frastanz, the builders erected a residential building on their parent's property. The stable building of the stately farmhouse was deconstructed and in its place, a three-story residential tower was placed. The building is a contemporary response to the surrounding farmhouses and part of a new ensemble of buildings.

Due to the ecological situation of the world, the wooden building was constructed entirely from the owner's own moon wood. All contractors, building materials and technology come from within a maximum radius of 50 kilometers. House in the Orchard is designed as a clear, straightforward, reduced structure. Structurally consistent, the solid wooden upper floors rest on three wooden columns coming up from the ground floor.

Due to the hillside location, the basement is built in solid construction with the visible part of the concrete base exposed. The rest of the building is a wooden structure.

Walls and ceilings are made of 24 centimeters thick solid spruce wood. The horizontally ribbed wooden façade is also made of spruce wood. Fir was used for windows, furniture and the acoustic ceiling, beech for the plank floors and stairs, and elm for the outdoor seating area furniture. In addition to wood, clay plaster and black steel are the other materials used. The client's great-grandparents had built the farmhouse from their own timber and then reforested the woods. From this wood, the great-granddaughter was able to build her own home. In this tradition, the forests have been reforested for future generations with 750 young trees.

This ecologically aware project stands out in a group of traditional buildings.

This two-story residential building for a family of four is located on the site of a former bakery in the south of Bielefeld, which was demolished in 2017 after it was given up by the bakery owner. In its place, the construction of a semi-detached house was planned instead. Completed so far is only one half of the duplex, the realization of the second half is still open. The roof and façade are clad in wood. The building thus takes up the materiality of its natural surroundings and blends harmoniously into the landscape that has characterized the site here for decades.

The new apartment building is located within the area that was occupied by the bakery business but with a much smaller area of land. The undeveloped areas have been largely transformed into green areas, partly lawns, partly a flower meadow, and also planted with more trees.

FAMILY HOME
BIELEFELD, GERMANY

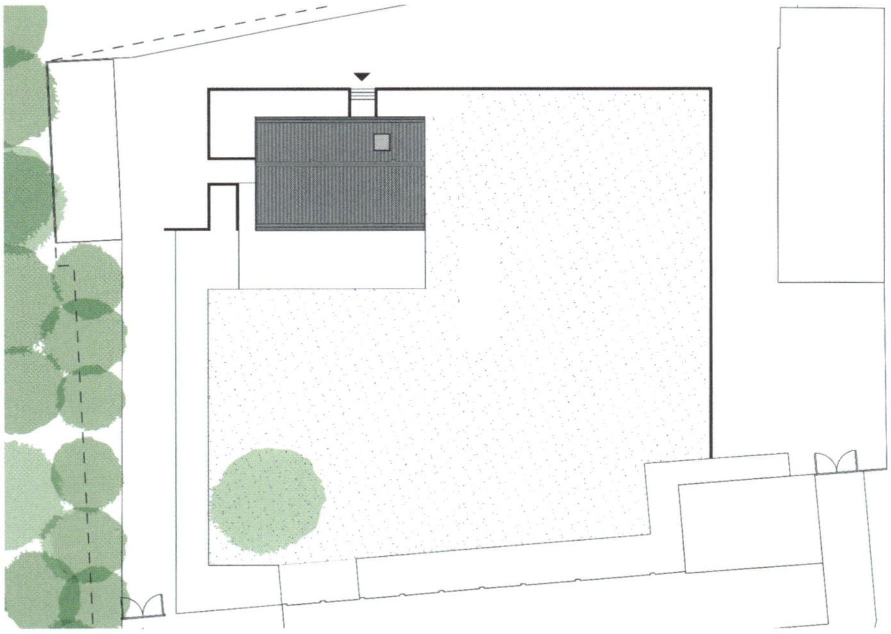

Architecture: Architekten Wannenmacher + Möller
Participating offices: figge ingenieure
Client: confidential
Year of completion: 2018
No. of bedrooms: 3 rooms
Gross floor area: 335 m²
Wood: 360 m² of charred larch used for façade and roof

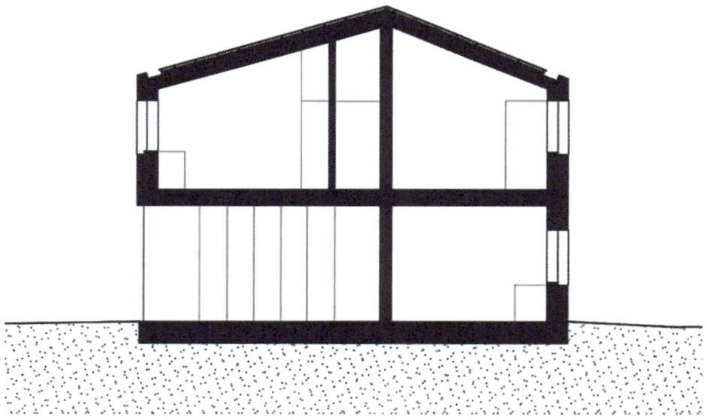

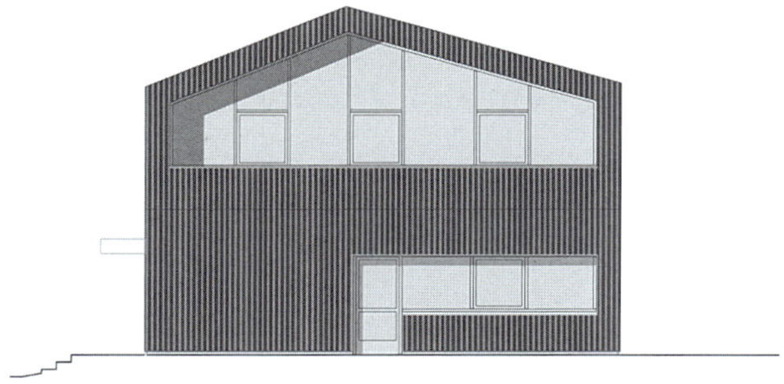

All bedrooms and bathrooms are located on the upper floor. The master bedroom faces north-east, allowing the morning sun to enter the room. The children's bedrooms face south-west, as does the living and dining area with kitchen, on the first floor. The latter can be spatially interconnected with the terrace in front of them through variably sliding window elements. A basement was not planned. Technical equipment and housekeeping items are housed in a room to the north-east. In front of its windows, the slats of the wooden façade run through without interruption, thus largely limiting visibility from the outside and maintaining privacy.

A cozy residence surrounded by greenery.

HOUSE SCHULZENDORF
SCHULZENDORF, GERMANY

The house for a family of four was built in a Brandenburg village on the outskirts of Berlin. The narrow and elongated lot, bordering a typical pine forest, had a significant impact on the design of the building.

The single-family house in Schulzendorf is a black solitaire on the outside. The interiors are light and the walls on the upper floor are covered with white glazed wood. For the façade, the architects used an old Japanese wood treatment technique. It was selectively flamed and charred, leaving the wood structure recognizable. This charred wood surface not only provides ecological protection against the weather but its shiny surface creates a unique sight, as it creates impressive effects depending on the daylight situation.

Architecture: Transstruktura
Client: confidential
Year of completion: 2019
No. of bedrooms: 4 rooms
Gross floor area: 228 m²
Wood: 106 m² of caboris spruce used for exterior wooden façade, 253 m² of white spruce used for interior wood planking

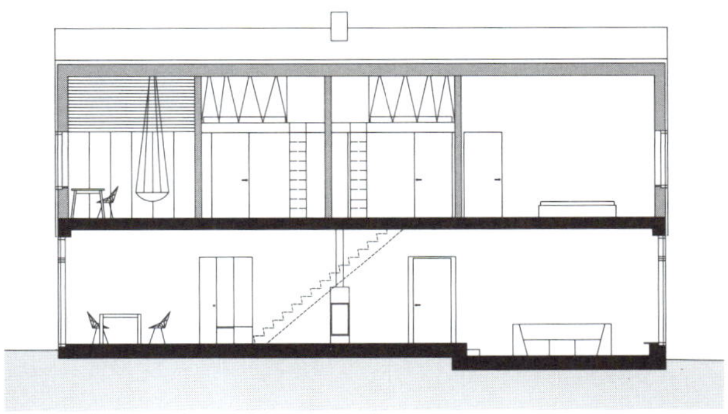

The dark, carbonated planks shimmer softly in the moon light.

The house was designed using a hybrid construction method. The solid first floor including the ceiling and middle wall up to the ridge purlin brings climatic inertia into the building and enables the light attic, which lies like a wooden casket on the concrete ceiling of the first floor. The vertical groove structure of the exterior plaster is based on the vertical wood planking of the upper floor. The walls and roof of the upper floor were designed in wood stud construction. On the room side, these are horizontally planked with white pine boards. The outer skin of the walls is boarded with carbonized pine boards.

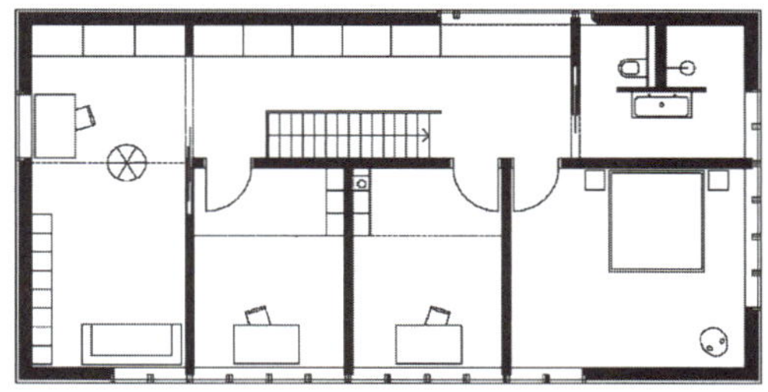

VILLA BALTICA
NIECHORZE, POLAND

The houses are located in Niechorze in the Western Pomerania Voivodeship, approximately 300 meters from the Baltic Sea and three kilometers from lake Liwia Łuża. Seven six-bed holiday cottages for rent have been built on the recreational site. One of the most important aspects during the design process was to provide the maximum possible privacy for future guests and an opening to the garden with a non-invasive localization of the parking spaces. Houses with a building area of just a little more than 35 square meters were designed in a very attractive style of a modern barn with a glazed front wall. The houses are located on the site in a way that allows them to open out to the garden from each of the glazed front elevations. The side and back walls are much more closed. A few windows placed to illuminate the rooms are located in such a way that they are not positioned right in view of the neighbor's windows.

Architecture: Z3Z Architekci
Interior design: Michał Niedostatkiewicz
Landscape design: Joanna Schindler
Client: Villa Baltica Niechorze
Year of completion: 2020
No. of bedrooms: 2 rooms each
Gross floor area: 50 m²
Wood: 280 m² of spruce used for façade, interior and construction each

On the ground floor, there is a bathroom, living room and open kitchen; on the first floor, two bedrooms and a toilet. The space inside is compact but comfortable. The shape of the house is simple and clean, due to this it looks good even in dense urban development and does not overwhelm. The façade is made of wooden boards in a vertical arrangement, the roof with a 45-degree angle is covered with a gray seam sheet. There is a small terrace in front of the glazed elevation.

A group of small homes that is perfect for a holiday visit.

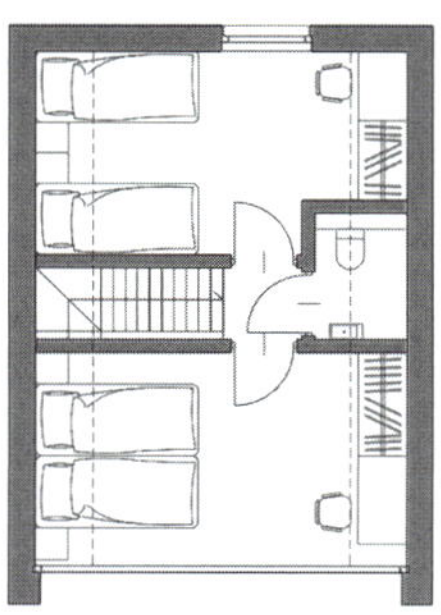

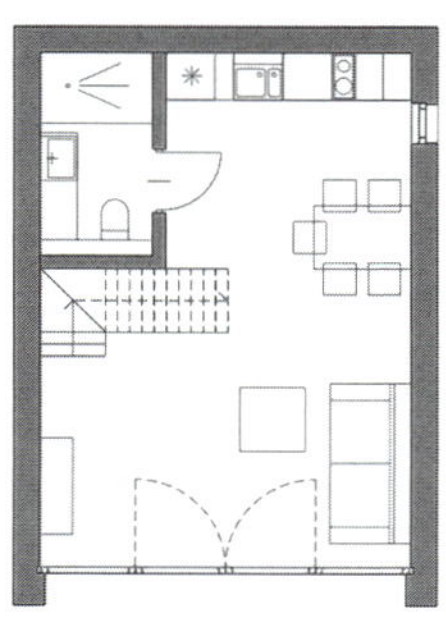

Architecture: FujiwaraMuro Architects
Client: confidential
Year of completion: 2019
No. of bedrooms: 3 rooms
Gross floor area: 78,7 m²
Wood: 34,5 m² of oak used for flooring and staircase, 69,7 m² of lauan plywood used for doors, 5,5 m² of Selangan batu used for deck

HOUSE IN SHUKUGAWA NISHINOMIYA, JAPAN

The living, dining, and kitchen areas of this house are located on the top two floors. The split-level design responds to the client's comment that family members tend to spend more time in shared living areas than in their bedrooms; split levels provide just the right amount of distance by separating lines of sight without fully closing off individual spaces.

The design pays particularly close attention to the views from various locations on these split levels. In the kitchen, windows offer vistas from both the right and left. The workspace behind the kitchen looks out on trees beyond neighboring houses and looks down on the property's own plantings. The dining table offers a vista of mountains. The view from the sofa features an open sky beyond the deck. From the Japanese-style room, one looks down from the street side on the garden and, from the opposite side, at the staircase, deck, and exterior landscape.

The central staircase of the split-levels leads to the shared living areas predominated by wood.

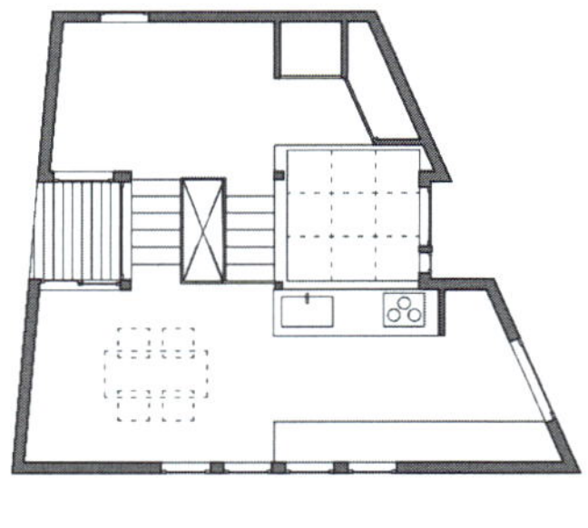

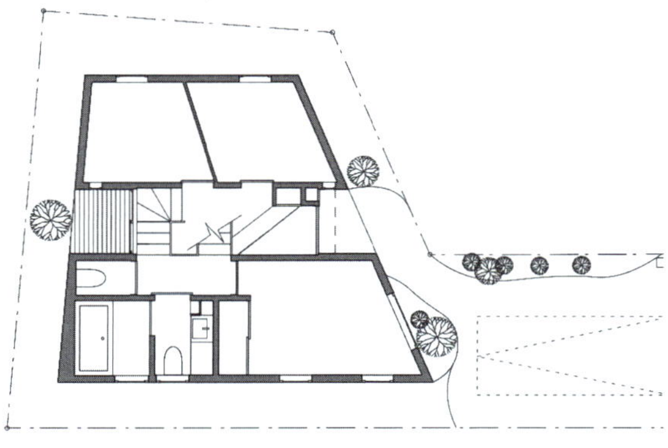

The entrance is located at the end of a curved approach with plantings along the side. Inside, a window directly opposite the entryway opens up the line of sight, while bedrooms, a walk-in closet, and several other private rooms are located to the left and right of the front hallway. Split levels are a classic way of alleviating the confined feeling in a small house, yet in this case they also became an opportunity for careful and deep consideration of the views from each part of the house.

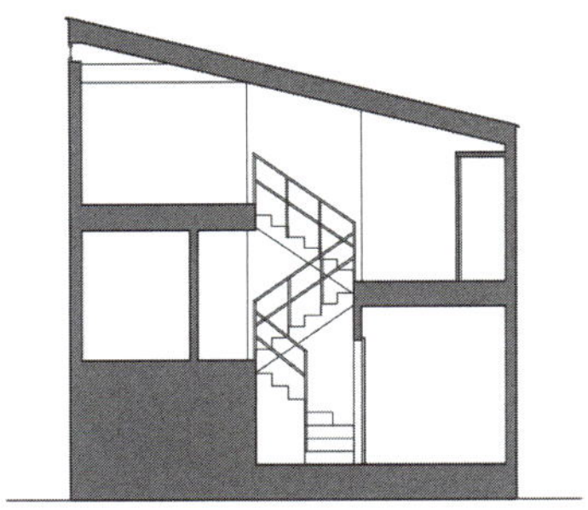

The family house was realized in the middle of greenery, on a 1,000 square meter plot. The basic approach was to live in a shell of natural building materials. Thus, a wooden building was realized, which defines sustainability not only through materiality but also allows flexible use in order to pursue a long life. From the larch wood façade to the load-bearing wooden structure to the oak wood paneling, floors and furniture in the interior, the majority of the house is built in wood.

The larch wood façade will turn gray over time to tell a story and is complemented by shading in the form of partial wooden slats over the windows. This creates detailed plays of light in the interior. Among other things, the house was aligned with the tree population – which means that the lush greenery also guarantees abundant shade in the summer.

MINIMALISM
KITZBÜHEL, AUSTRIA

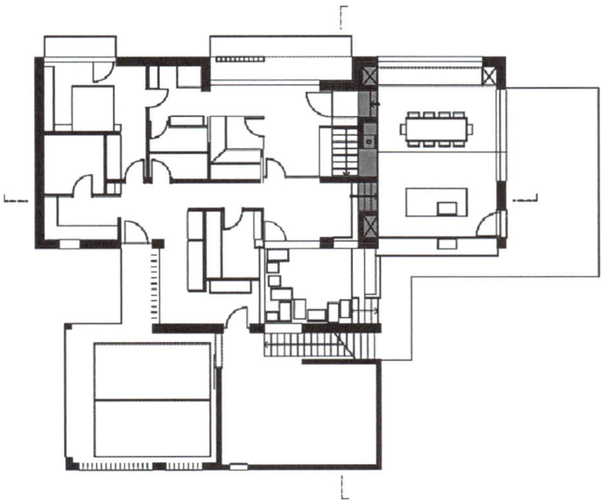

Architecture: Snow Architektur
Client: confidential
Year of completion: 2021
No. of bedrooms: 4 rooms
Gross floor area: 450 m²
Wood: spruce used for wall construction, ceilings and roof truss, 310 m² of larch used for façade formwork, 350 m² of oak used for roof soffit, wall paneling and floors

The single-family house offers a life in the wood trunk.

Seatings directly next to the windows give the dwellers inside a feeling of being outside.

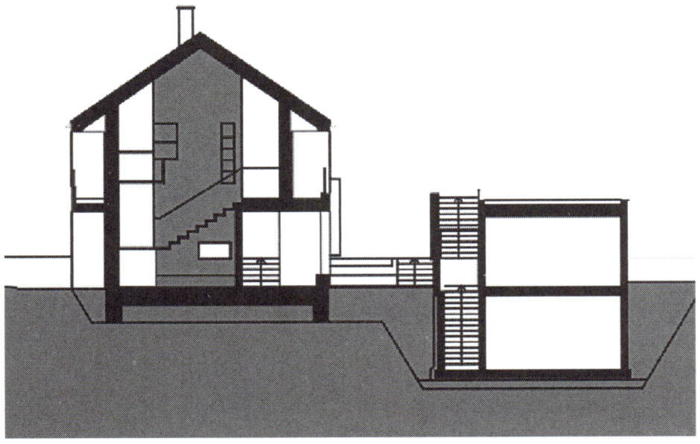

The fireplace integrated into the exposed concrete core efficiently supports the natural storage capacity of the concrete. In addition, the combination of wood and concrete creates playful details that liven up the minimalist building. Furthermore, the client's desire for the feeling of living outside was implemented through generous glass elements. These glass elements make the interior of the wooden building shine with brightness and allow views from east to west, blending the boundaries of inside to outside.

HOUSE W1T
TULLN, AUSTRIA

West of the center of Tulln, a spacious residential building is concealed behind a closed façade. With access from the street in the north, the narrow structure extends from north to south. On the street side, the ground floor, made of individual concrete blocks, and the wooden structure above it present themselves as two clearly separated volumes. The ground-level blocks are offset from each other in such a way that on the street side an incised entrance area and on the garden side an incised loggia are created. In between, a generous but differentiated living space was created. Towards the south, the building opens up more and more and is finally oriented completely towards the garden.

As soon as one enters the building, a view axis opens up into the greenery. The glazed living space allows the exterior and interior to merge and creates an open atmosphere. The children's rooms on the upper floor are nested together by raised levels under the gable. The bedroom and bathroom are connected by an incised terrace. It allows light to flood into the interior and provides an additional hidden outdoor space.

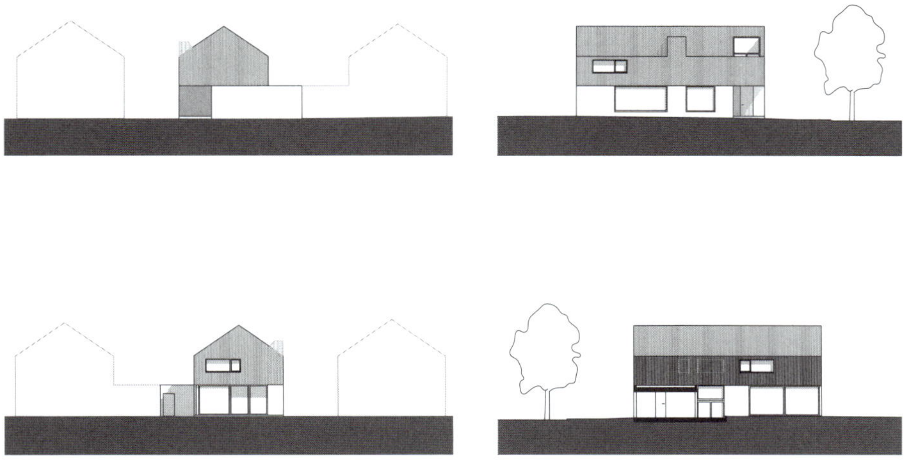

Architecture: juri troy architects
Client: confidential
Year of completion: 2020
No. of bedrooms: 4 rooms
Gross floor area: 265 m²
Wood: solid wood elements / CLT used for construction silver fir used for interior finishes, solid silver fir used for interior doors and furniture, oiled white ash used for flooring, native coniferus wood used for window frames, untreated silver fir used for façade, larch used for terrace, soft wood fiber used for isolation

The ground floor and basement are concrete structures. This raw character is obvious on the entrance floor, where exposed concrete and soft wooden surfaces of silver fir and white oiled ash meet. The upper floor is a solid wooden structure placed on a concrete base. The construction principle is carried on to the outside via the façades made of fiber concrete panels at the bottom and vertical wooden battens at the top.

A geothermal heat pump ensures a sustainable energy concept, which is supported additionally by controlled living space ventilation with heat recovery.

A modern fusion of concrete and timber.

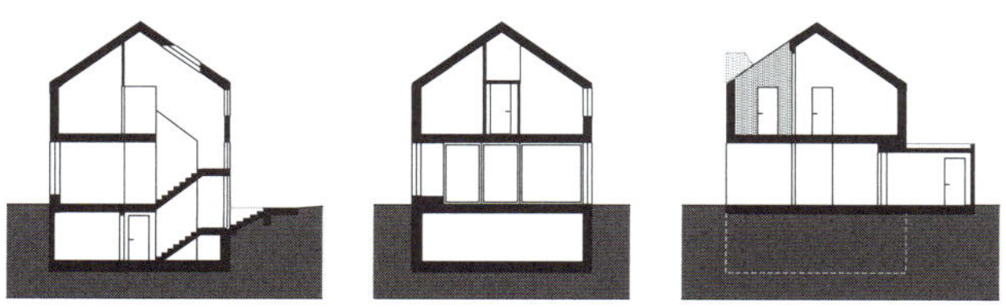

Architecture: SKA Sibylle Kramer Achitekten
Client: confidential
Year of completion: 2019
No. of bedrooms: 5 rooms
Gross floor area: 387 m²
Wood: silver fir used for facçade, spruce used for construction and interior, oak used for flooring and window frames

HOUSE AT THE LAKE
NEHMTEN, GERMANY

The aim of the House at the Lake was to build a modern family vacation home that fits into the scene of the surrounding nature and buildings. Emphasis was placed on a design that aligns with the historical traditions of building in Northern Germany, without trying to replicate certain historical styles. Thus, the cubature of the new residential building corresponds exactly to the old barn that previously stood on this site. In the spirit of carefully handling the site, the architects placed particular emphasis on preserving the courtyard situation and the typical local rural character.

A surrounding horizontal visible joint divides the vertical formwork and quotes the guidance of barn doors. The choice of material is also in line with the origin and the idea of sustainability. The new building was constructed in a resource-saving and material-friendly manner as a prefabricated wood-frame structure with a solid, untreated board-stack ceiling and a façade made of native silver fir. The purlin roof was given a covering typical of a barn. Borrowings from typical elements of barn construction characterize the appearance of the new building: Via flush sliding shutters that are identical in materiality and construction to the façade, the house can close itself completely against views, solar or thermal radiation.

A modern take on historical barn-building styles with nature in mind.

At these moments, its use as a residential building is no longer apparent – the closed shell is perceived as a barn again. The sparingly used floor-to-ceiling windows are placed in such a way that they set the stage for nature, the actual star, and direct the gaze there. Native herbs and wildflowers have been reseeded to establish themselves in the 6,000 square meters of pasture that was once used for agriculture. The wildflower meadows are the habitat for many animals and form an important contribution to biodiversity.

INDIGO TANJA & JOS
BARCHEM, NETHERLANDS

The Indigo Tanja & Jos home consists of separate, prefabricated elements that are assembled on site. These elements are characterized by a "moment resisting"-bend that not only allows for a free layout of the floor plan but at the same time yields a beautiful, curved line between the wall and roof. The size and roof inclination of the elements themselves can, within certain margins, also be adjusted. The elements are made of beams from laminated wood and filled with cellulose, a bio-based insulation material. Numerous options are possible for finishing the roof, façade and interior.

For this home, the owners, Tanja and Jos, were contributing to the design process with sketches as well. The house has a clever spatial layout: The living area and the sleeping house in the back are separated by a spacious hall where Tanja and Jos can organize cozy events, like lectures and room concerts. This zoning also yields smart, separated climate zones. The foundation of this house consists of prefabricated concrete beams and pier blocks that are placed on the underlying sandy soil. In this way, the house, which stands on lease land, does not leave any traces should it ever be removed. On top of that, the floor below is insulated around the edges only: the thermal mass of the ground under the house is utilized. This provides extra cooling capacity in the summer and flattens out the heat curve in the winter, due to the buffering capacity of the sand.

Architecture: Woonpioniers
Client: confidential
Year of completion: 2019
No. of bedrooms: 4 rooms
Gross floor area: 141 m²
Wood: laminated timber used for construction, larch beams used for glass façade, stained douglas used for façade

A sculptured response
to the site's topography.

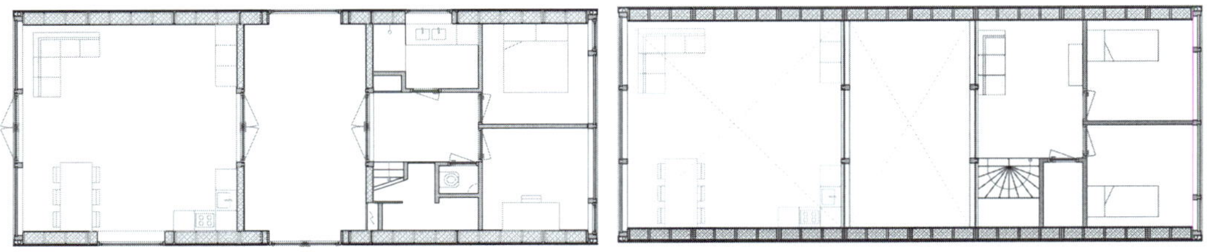

Indigo allows the owners to make a meaningful contribution to their own home in the design process.

Indigo runs fully on electricity, a clean choice, provided that the required electricity is generated sustainably. Because the surrounding trees give a lot of shade, in this case, the energy is generated within a collective project nearby. The underfloor heating, which can also cool, is powered by an air-to-water heatpump.

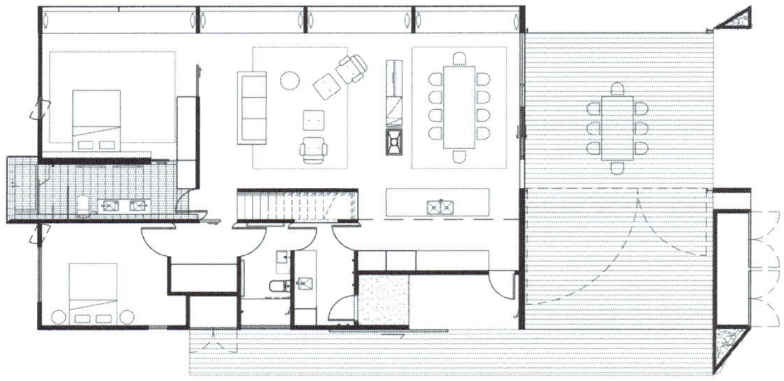

Architecture: FMD Architects
Client: confidential
Year of completion: 2020
No. of bedrooms: 3 rooms
Gross floor area: 199 m²
Wood: birch plywood used for interior walls and joinery

COOPWORTH
BRUNY ISLAND, AUSTRALIA

Nestled in the rural surrounds of Bruny Island, Tasmania, Coopworth is a contemporary interpretation of a country farmhouse. The site's inhabitants of Coopworth sheep, the wide-ranging views of the water and mountain ranges beyond, as well as the weathering red lead shacks dotted over the island provide an ever-changing landscape with which the house converses. The footprint of the house is consciously constrained to maximize arable land yet maintains generosity in its thoughtful internal arrangement.

Inspired by Australian verandah sleepouts, this residence offers a cozy fireplace.

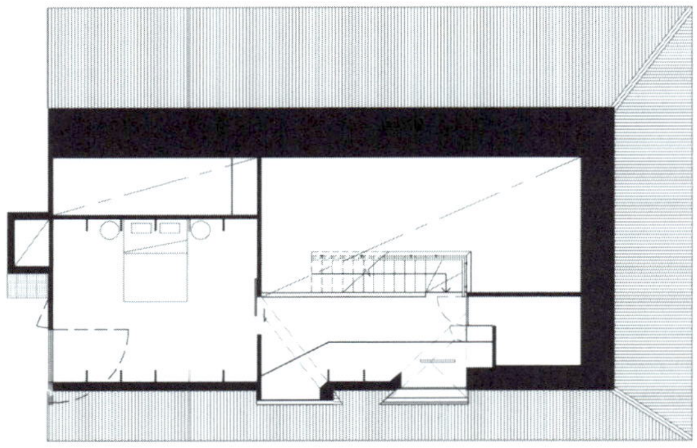

While designed to accommodate two principal occupants, the house can be opened up to host family and friends through creative interpretations of Australian verandah sleepouts and caravan bunk beds. Frameless windows are pushed to the edge of the floorplate to embrace wild winds and rains – at once immersed in the beauty and brutality of the weather and well protected from it.

MARRA MARRA SHACK
BEROWA, AUSTRALIA

In the building of the Marra Marra Shack reclaimed materials from the area of the Dyirabun River in Australia were used. This links the new-build home to the long history of the site. The house is built using timber pillars made out of repurposed 200-year-old electrical posts, giving a new life to the Ironbark timber. Spotted gum timber growing in the Darug region is used for the beams of the ceiling and floor. The details and furniture are made of repurposed turpentine timber from the old jetty built by the settlers on the banks of the creek.

The stepped longitudinal section in conjunction with a tightly arranged structural grid acknowledges the steeply sloping site upon which the house is located on. The interior of the dwelling is entirely focused on one single large north-facing window orientated towards the creek edge. The window is split in half and can be hoisted upwards using counter weights, allowing the landscape into the tranquil timber lined interior space. Two small rooms open to a patio protected from the wild nature surrounding the building.

Architecture: Leopold Banchini Architects
Client: confidential
Year of completion: 2022
No. of bedrooms: 2 rooms
Gross floor area: 67 m²
Wood: ironbark timber used for pillars, gum timber used for beems for ceiling and floor, turpentine timber used for details and furniture

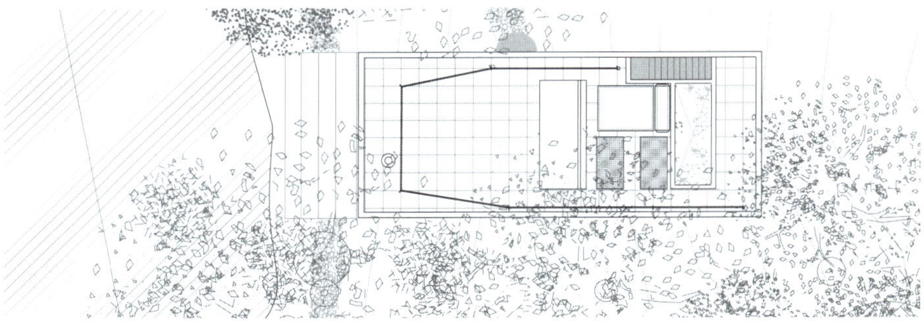

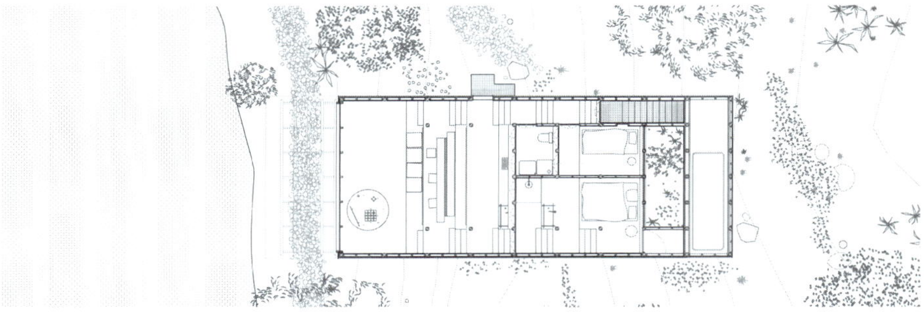

Above the house, the flat roof offers a large terrace in the tree canopy. The house is entirely built in timber; only the façade is covered by thin fire-resistant fiber cement sheets. The footings are pinned to the underlying sandstone bedrock, avoiding the need for heavy concrete footings and reducing the impact on the site as well as the number of trades and machinery required during the construction process to a bare minimum. Both solar energy and water are collected on the roof and stored on site, making the house fully self-sustainable.

This build was designed with the Aboriginal history of the Darug in mind.

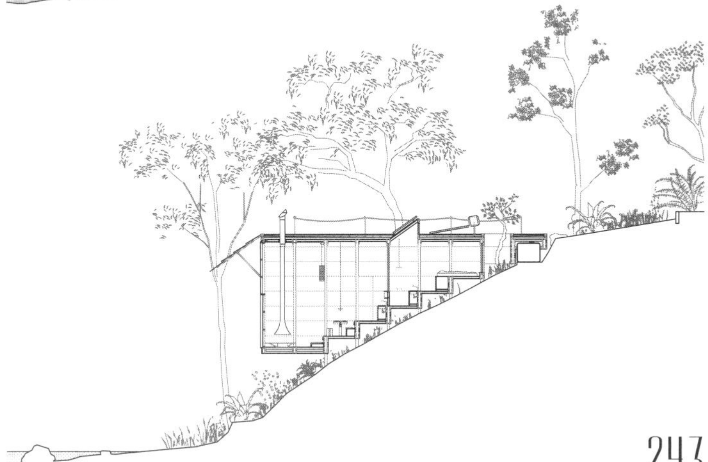

SOTTILE HOUSE
SÃO PAULO, BRAZIL

As the name suggests, Sottile House is about subtlety, petrified in an architectural gesture in which a fifty-meter prism sits on the hill to observe the mass of vegetation that presents the view to which the residence is oriented.

The project was developed in an unconventional way, as the hall and the main access are located in a private block. The dark structure is designed in a rhythm that frames the warmth of the wood with which the private suites are wrapped. Modern colors stand out against the natural wood frame and walls, matching the surrounding trees and integrating themselves within the surrounding landscape. A large swimming pool over the full length of the backside corresponds with a water feature inside the ground floor.

Architecture: Felipe Caboclo Arquitetura
Client: confidential
Year of completion: 2022
No. of bedrooms: 6 rooms
Gross floor area: 1,519 m²
Wood: accoya used for walls and most of interior

A helical staircase leads up and connects the floors in an elegant manner.

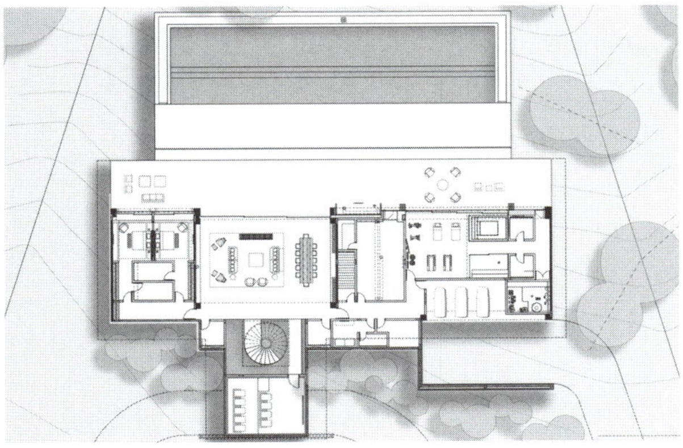

From the main hall, a sculptural spiral staircase leads over a reflecting water feature to the two-story social area, which integrates with the exterior with a large transverse strip; materialities that are also challenged by the juxtaposition of stone and water elements. On the subtlety of the unification of opposites, the creation of blank spaces in the full, the architecture is born which, in its simplicity, is complete.

CASA MAGUE
MALINALCO, MEXICO

The house is built in a town with a strong pre-Hispanic and Hispanic heritage. The starting point was a small house built in the 1970s located next to the archaeological zone, the mountain and in the middle of the historic center. The owners wanted to give value to their land full of trees. Different specific volumes, adjusted within the architecture, were placed to avoid the roots and branches of the trees. To achieve this, the architects had to constantly modify foundations, planes and the height of the volumes.

The house was intended for a family who wanted to use it for long vacations. But they also wanted to have additional income by renting it out on Airbnb. That's why all the interiors, designed by Paola Cueli, are very warm but not very personal. The house functions like a small boutique hotel, with different spaces for shelter or meeting. A kitchen-dining room offers seating for 20 people in glass for dining surrounded by plum trees. The different spaces are a combination of places to be close to nature, contrasted with places to be with family and friends. The social areas – jacuzzi, living rooms, fire pit, and dining room, are planned for cooking, resting and enjoying nature – make up an architectural space that blurs physical boundaries.

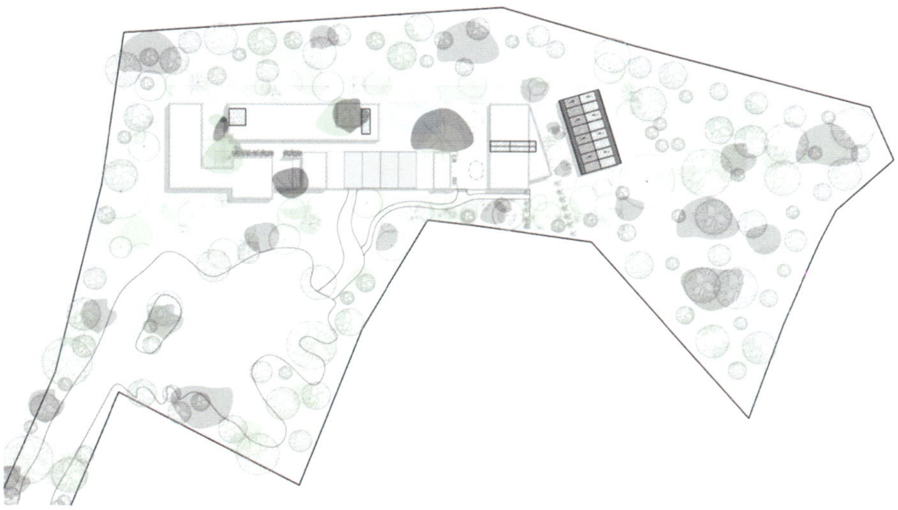

Architecture: Mauricio Ceballos x Architects
Interior design: Paola Cueli
Client: confidential
Year of completion: 2019
No. of bedrooms: 4 rooms
Gross floor area: 270 m²
Wood: chukum used for finish of the walls and swimming pools with a smooth texture

Sensual textures make the users experience the project through different spaces interrupted by trees and courtyards.

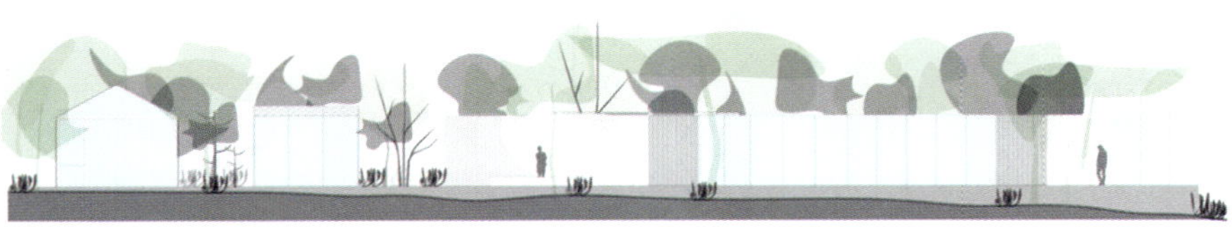

The house uses local materials, such as wood, and the outdoor living room is an interpretation of a pyramid but made with a parametric design of wood. This concept goes beyond materiality, especially in the relationship between the interior and exterior. Although the design mimics nature, the tree canopies become a space to feel, look, listen and smell. Symbolic quotes reference the archaeological zone and the Mesoamerican cosmovision.

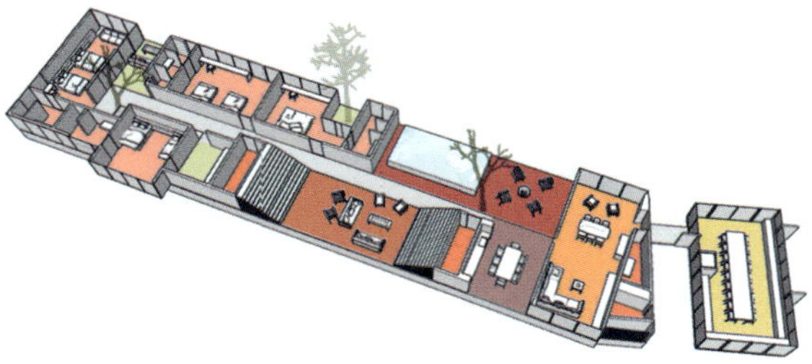

The biggest challenge was to integrate the project with the existing plum trees, without touching any trees, branches or roots.

INDEX

PICTURE CREDITS

Front cover: Lukas Schaller
Back cover (from left to right): Paola Cueli , Celso Mellani

10–15 Jehann Gisli Brunk www.instagram.com/jehann_gisli
16–19 Nigel Young www.nigelyoung.co.uk
20–23 Jos. Campos www.josecamposphotographer.com
24–27 Tiago Casanova
28–31 DI Bruno Moser www. archimos.at
32–35 Lukas Glatt
36–40 Martin Sommerschield www.kuvio.com
41 Minna Kivinen www.instagram.com/minnaflintstone
42–45 Michael Moran www. moranstudio.com
46-47,
48 a. Stefan Müller-Naumann www.architektur-fotograf-muenchen.de
48 b.,
49 r. Bert Heinzelmeier www.bertheinzlmeier.de
50–53 Albrecht Schnabel www.albrecht-schnabel.com
54–57 Bernd Ducke www.bernddducke.de
58–63 Andre Nazareth www.andrenazareth.com
64–67 Markus Rohrbacher www.markusrohrbacher.com
68–71 Toomas Tuul www.instagram.com/toomastuul
72–75 Edgard Schmeichel www.hopetoun.de
76–81 Nicolas Cruz
82–85 Florin Lang, Luzern www.florinlang.ch
86–89 Kaku Ohtaki www.cak1104.myportfolio.com
90–93 Andriy Bezuglov
94–99 Marcin Mularczyk www.fotoradarmm.pl
100–103 David Schreyer www.schreyerdavid.com
104–107 Bojune Kwon
108–111 Markus Guhl www.architekturfotograf-markus-guhl.com
112–115 Juri Troy www.juritroy.com
116–121 Václav Novák www.vaclavnovak.com
122–125 Erich Spahn www.erich-spahn.de
126–129 VC www.instagram.com/v.ee_chin
130–133 Edgard Schmeichel www.hopetoun.de
134–135,
136 l. Aistė Rakauskaitė www. instagram.com/aiste.rakauskaite
136 r., 137 Edvinas Ganusauskas
138–141 Serge Grard www.grard.ch
142–147 Kazunori Fujimoto www.jutok.jp
148–151 Oki Hiroyuki www.instagram.com/oki.hiroyuki.47
152–153,
154 l.,
155 r. Dan Cardon www.danjcardon.com
154–155 Jim Westphalen www.jimwestphalenfineart.com
156–161 Ruben P. Bescós www.instagram.com/rubenpb
162–167 Christian Richters
168–171 Celia Uhalde www.celiauhalde.com
172–177 Philipp Mürdter www.philippmuerdter.de
178–181 Markus Guhl www.architekturfotograf-markus-guhl.com
182–185 Roland Halbe www.rolandhalbe.eu
186–191 Celso Mellani www.mellani.com.br
192–195 Vincent Leroux / Jean-Luc Guérin
196–199 Adolf Bereuter www.adolfbereuter.com
200–203 Csaba Mester www.mester-fotografie.de
204–207 Klemens Renner www. klemensrenner.com
208–211 Marta Misiecka www.facebook.com/artphotomartamisiecka
212–215 Naoki Yoshikawa / dig photograph www.photo-dig.com
216–221 Lukas Schaller www.lukasschaller.at
222–225 Juri Troy www.juritroy.com
226–229 SKA Sibylle Kramer Achitekten BDA www.kramer-architekten.de
230–235 Henny van Belkom www.vanbelkomproducties.nl
236–239 Dianna Snape www.diannasnape.com
240–243 Rory Gardiner www.rory-gardiner.com
244–247 Leonardo Finotti www.leonardofinotti.com
248–253 Paola Cueli